G & G:

Live With No Edits

By

Londonaire Visions

A NOVEL FOR YOUNG FATHERS

G & G
Live With No Edits

This story is a message to all the fathers that weren't give guidelines to fatherhood, to the the fathers that never had real role models, and especially for the fathers that were raised by all women. This book is to teach you why your presence is important for your children, and the things that you should teach your children. I hope you enjoy.

LONDONAIRE VISIONS

Fatherhood is important.

Being Black in America: March 19, 2015

It was a long day for Keith Young today. Keith is better known by his family and friends as G. While at work, G's co-worker thought it would be funny to mention to the manager that G was on his phone the entire shift and not working like he was supposed to be. The manager didn't have a smile on his face as he requested that G speak with him privately in his office.

On the way to the office, G is questioning God about what could possibly be happening in his life right now. The rent is due, but he doesn't have all of his money together. Then on top of that, his Grandmother could possibly be slowly dying from cancer as we speak right now.

His truck just blew out on him. He immediately purchased a three thousand dollar transmission because he already knows the feeling of having independent freedom of owning his own vehicle. You could have a million cousins and five friends, and it's still as hard to find a ride. Isn't it?

They walk into his cold office. It's kind of dark too. You know when the walls are dirty in a small room and it gives the whole room a dirty brown tint evenly reflecting off of the dusty light bulb. That's what G sees right now.

Mr. Kells: Mr. Young, I am going to have to let you go. This is the third time this week you have been called into my office because you can't stay off that phone. Why are you young kids so attached to y'all phones so much?

G: With all due respect sir, I am no kid. I am a Young man with responsibilities. While I do apologize for being on my phone, all of my work has been completed thoroughly. Like I told you before, my grandma is sick with cancer. Every once in a while throughout the day she sends me text messages. I would like to respond to her immediately because what if this is the last time that I will ever be able to physically contact her, and I didn't respond? She's my grandma, man. She raised me. I don't want her to die yet. I need at least twelve good years. It's so much I want to do with her.

G sits there and cries for a second. Then Mr. Kells responds.

Mr. Kells: I'm sorry to hear that, but you're fired, Mr. Young. I have to stick to protocol. What kind of example would I be setting for the other employees? They don't know what you are going through. All they see is an employee breaking the rules. They don't think it is okay for you to think that you have special privileges. If I let you stay, then the others won't take me seriously when I enforce the rules.

I did not create the rule book but I get paid a fair hourly rate to enforce the rules. But from my sincere standpoint, I am truly sorry to hear about your grandmother. My grandmother just passed away a year ago today, and it hurts like hell. But you just keep praying, and hang on. God just might actually grant you those extra years. Please don't allow this storm to discourage you. It gets better.

G: Well. Thank you for the opportunity when you hired me. I truly appreciate that.

Mr. Kells: You are more than welcome. I knew you would be a good asset to the team. Unfortunately, you set one bad example, and it terminated your employment, but hey. This is not the end of the world. I loved that shirt you had on the other day. I heard you say that you designed it?

G responds smiling incredibly hard.

G: Oh yeah. I love coming up with new creative logos and art designs for my clothes. I just like that I'm the only one in the world with pants like this and shirt like that. You know what I mean?

Mr. Kells: That's how I felt when my son was born. He was one of a kind indeed. I was twenty-five when he got here, and none of my friends had babies then. I thought I was so cool. I would show him to the world. We would walk around and talk to all kinds of people just because I want to express just how happy I was to be his father. I loved that little boy. But now I love the man that he has become. He is the kind of guy that demonstrates greatness with everything he does. You take your desire to create and design, and you nourish it as if it's your own son, and you will be able to start your own business soon. Just make sure you're prepared. It's better to plan ahead.

G: Thank you. I will. Actually have a son on the way. He's almost here. I guess I can raise them like brothers.

 G firmly shakes his hand, stands up, and walks out of Mr. Kells' office. On the way out of the door, G's girlfriend, Peaches, calls.

Peaches: Hey, G! Are you off yet?

G: Oh, I'm off alright.

Peaches : Great! How was your day?

G: It was actually good and bad at the same time. How was yours?

Peaches: It was alright. Would you like to go to Cold Stone to get some ice cream? I think that would cheer you up a little bit.

G: I'm not going to lie to you, Peaches. I don't have any money right now. I just got fired right before you called me, and I just had to spend three thousand dollars to get a transmission for my truck yesterday. I spent my rent money on fixing that raggedy truck.. But you know what, I will ask my brother to use his food stamp card to get you some ice cream from the grocery store, and I'll take you to the park to eat it. Would you like that?

Peaches: Baby, you should show a little more appreciation for that truck. That's probably why it gives you so many problems. Learn how to appreciate even the small things, because every situation has a solution. It's no use in getting worked up about it. God always makes a way. Like now, I will pay your rent this month. So that is one out of none of the things that you have to worry about.

G: Well thank you for the lesson, and thank you so much for the blessings.

Peaches: No problem, How long before you get home? I can just pick you up from your house.

G: Thank you, Baby. But I should be ready around seven o'clock. I have to stop by Quanita's house first to check on the baby. I told you I caught her smoking weed one day last week?

Peaches: What? Are you serious, G!!? Look, I knew what I was signing up for when I agreed to be your girlfriend after you told me that your ex girl was pregnant. But you didn't tell me that she was totally irresponsible like that!!

G: I completely agree with you. That's why I'm popping up over there to see what else she is doing behind my back. I just have a bad feeling about her, and I need her to hurry up and give birth to my son so I know that he is okay under my care.

Peaches: Well while he is in her care, all we can do is pray for God to protect your little boy from any hurt, harm, or danger. Thank you in advance, Lord.

G: Thank you, Lord. Alright. I'll call you when I'm on the way home.

Peaches: Alright, G. *She disconnects the phone call.*

G gets in the car and begins to pray.

G: God, I know that I haven't always been the nicest person in the world, but I am asking that you protect me from what's about to come because something doesn't feel right. Like. I don't know what it is I'm feeling, but I know that I don't like it. Please God. If it doesn't kill me, please God, allow it to make me stronger. Thank you. I love you, God.

Five minutes later, G pulls up to his baby mama's house. She is eight months pregnant with G's son, Kenneth Young. Kenneth will be both G and Quinita's first child. G is twenty and she's twenty-seven years old. She lives alone, in Kayton Holmes project housing. G has a key to her house, so when he walks in the door, he finds his baby mama, Quinita, blasting NBA Young Boy, Temporary Time, as loud as her boombox will allow. She's drinking straight from a full bottle of pure Grey Goose. She has a Backwood of Georgia grown weed, and she has two lines of cocaine on the glass coffee table, just waiting for her to sniff it up.

G loses his mind! Normally G keeps his composure during unexpected occurrences , but after everything he has been enduring for the past couple days, he spazzes out.

G & G: LIVE WITH NO EDITS

G: What is this, Quinita!

G aggressively snatches the bottle and the joint from her hand. He wants to punch her dead in the middle of her face for disrespecting his son like that. She's eight months pregnant with his child, and she's deciding to give her son drugs and liquor. Is she serious?

G: I'm sick and tired of this, Quinita. All you wanna do is sit on your behind and beg for my money. I used to not know what you were doing with all that money. Now I do. You're smoking and sniffing it up, WHILE CARRYING MY SON! The second you deliver my baby, I'm through with you, on God! I just came over here to make sure that my son was over here living a healthy life and you're over here trying to kill him!

G burst out into tears,

G: If my son dies, you die, and I mean that!

G found Quinita sniffing up cocaine once, before she got pregnant. When he questioned her about it, she told him she doesn't do it often. She only does it when she's extremely stressed out. G used to care about her dearly, so he begged her to promise him that she'll find another stress reliever, and she did for a while. But after they had broken up, she felt like she didn't want the baby if she couldn't have the man. Those were her intentions the entire time.

G made it clear that he didn't want to be with her after he realized that she didn't encourage him to be any better. She didn't motivate him to do anything. She was not even wasn't moved by his motivation or his drive. She didn't seem to support him the way that he was looking for in a partner. She begged a lot. She didn't teach him anything, and she was hard to be taught.

He tried voicing his concerns, but nothing changed. He decided to separate himself from her as a relationship partner when she was three months pregnant. He was still coming around to check on her from time to time, but then he met Peaches a month later.

Peaches was a fun girl. She was a refreshing rebound for him. He went from being totally miserable with the simple thought of going over to his girlfriend, Quinta's house to going out every night with this young, fly chick that made him laugh all day. He felt good about her because she was about her business. They both never verbally committed to being in a relationship, but it's kind of implied.

Ever since he met Peaches, the number of times that he visits Quinta has decreased. For the past two months, G just calls to see how everything is going with the baby. She's been feeling abandoned. Now they are both standing in her living looking each other in the eyes, and no one can say a word.

G grabs all the drugs off her table and shoves them in his left pocket.

G: I will be back.

He walks out of the door and slams it so hard that the vibrations break the glass coffee table, while Quinita calls the police.

Operator: 911, what's your emergency?

Quinita: *crying* My baby's father just hit me and left! He has a left pocket full of drugs, and he's very dangerous!

Operator : What's your name and location ma'am?

Quinita: Quinita Topple. 704 Gwinnett St. His name is Keith Young. He's twenty years old, and he's wearing a brown Herty work jacket and some black work shoes. He left his keys so he's walking somewhere in the projects.

Operator: We have an officer already posted on Gwinnett Street. I am going to let him know to be on the look-out for a man that fits your description. And I'm sending an officer to you right now.

Quinita: Thank you so much! *She hangs the phone up, stops fake crying, and she laughs* That'll show your controlling behind not to mess with me anymore! I'm a grown woman! He's always thinking he can tell me what to do, but he doesn't even love me anymore. All he wants is his baby. I don't care about him or his child. Let's see how he controls anything behind those bars, because that's where he's going tonight! Buster!

G & G: LIVE WITH NO EDITS

G is walking down toward Burger King coming down MLK street when the officer jumps out of his car.

White officer: Hey! Get on the ground now! *G takes off running* Looks like I got a little action tonight. *He hops back in the car, and he gets close enough to, BOOM! The officer shoots G in his left leg*

G screams and falls to the ground*

The officer laughs.

Officer: Got em!

He jumps out of the car.

Officer: So you like to beat up on women, huh, loser?

G: What are you talking about?!

The white officer slaps G across the mouth with his pistol.

Officer: Shut up. You are not allowed to me! I hate men who beat up on women. I like to see you try to beat me up, Punk, I bet you can't even stand up.

He goes directly to G's left pocket for the drugs. He laughs.

Officer: Looks like you're going to be spending a few years at my playpen now, boy. You just might turn out to be somebody's little girlfriend and then you'll see just how fun it is to get beat up by your boyfriend.

While he is handcuffing G, he is reading him his required Miranda rights because if he does not recite them, he does not have the right to arrest G.

Officer: You have the right to remain silent. Anything you say can and will be used against you in the court of law. You have the right to an attorney. If you cannot afford one, one will be appointed to you by the court. With these rights in mind, are you willing to talk with me about the charges against you?

G: I didn't lay a finger on that girl. She's lying, and that stuff isn't mine! It's hers! Check the finger prints! *spits blood near the officer's foot*

Officer: Silence! *He kicks G, and he breaks G's jaw. *

That night, G was escorted to the hospital to be treated for his broken jaw and his gunshot wound. He was in so much pain, and he kept questioning God, asking him what did he do to deserve the treatment that he received tonight. He wanted answers, and he wanted them now! Anybody that knows God, knows that there is a plan taking place within all this chaos. Stay steadfast. Keep your mind stayed on God, and this too shall come to pass.

A week later, he has to attend court for a hearing. He feels like he deserves to be released because he knows and Quinita definitely knows that he was wrongfully convicted. **Judge Brogan:** So it says here that Mr. Keith Young, has verbally and physically abused his now ex-girlfriend, who is also pregnant with his child. I can't tell you how many of these cases that I receive on a daily basis. I honestly believe you, Ms. Topple, and I am very apologetic that you had to endure such hardship. I pray that the trauma from this event does not harm your baby in any form.

G speaks to his public defender loud enough for the judge to hear.

G: He's siding with her because she's a pregnant woman. Mommy's lie too.

Judge Brogan: I did not ask for your lies. What does she have to lie and say you hit her for if it's not true.

G: With all due respect, your honor, the woman is a compulsive liar. I walked in...

Judge Brogan: Save your lies and you are not to speak to me. That is why you were assigned a public defender, but right now, I am talking, I do not tolerate any form of domestic violence. Women, especially the pregnant ones, deserve men who will protect and care for them. They don't deserve a man who will verbally abuse them. Words can hurt, you know. And they definitely do not need a man beating up on them, like some punching bag. So from here on out, you will be serving the next five years in federal prison. They will ship you out of the county immediately after being released from here.

G: You didn't even hear what I had to say! I am an innocent man! I do not deserve this! I didn't even touch this girl at all! Quinita, tell the truth!

Judge Brogan: Get him and his rude outburst out of my courtroom now! They all claim to be innocent. Court is adjourned.

Immediately, a loud scream is released from the plaintiff's side of the courtroom! The whole courtroom is in panic mode as the cries of agony are coming from Quinita's petite, pregnant body. She's dripping wet caused by her water breaking, and she just experienced a contraction for the first time in her life. G pleads to the court to be there for the birth of his son.

G: Please! I need to see my baby be born! I need to see my little man take his first breath. I need to see that my son is okay. I need to see my son.

He bursted out into tears as the officer drags him out of the courtroom.

An hour later, G takes an hour ride out to Reidsville Prison which is a little over an hour away from his hometown, Savannah, Georgia. He walks in his cell to see a black man with long gray locs as his cellmate.

G & G: LIVE WITH NO EDITS

Sanka: *says with a thick Jamaican accent* Waa gwaan, Young King?

G: Wassup?

Sanka : Mi name Sanka. What's your name?

G: G.

Sanka: How old are you?

G : Twenty.

Sanka : I'm sixty. Mi been in here since I was your age.

G's whole life flashes before his eyes. G thinks of the time when he was five years old. He was a little grown boy who took on the role of the responsible brother. By seven he understands that his brothers weren't as advanced as him because both of their mothers weren't as present as his mother was, and their dad was nowhere to be found if you weren't a junkie in the street.

G understood that early, so he asked his mother to pick his brothers up whenever she had the mental capacity to deal with three wild and adventurous boys under one roof. She picked them up all the time. They kept her entertained, and she loved every second of it.

Once G turned nine, his whole life changed without a warning, his Grandfather, Tyrone Cotton passed away, and they were extremely close. Grandpa had spent his last nine years teaching G everything he knew and experienced. G was his right hand man, and one thing he didn't do around his right hand man was frown nor complain. He smiled the whole time. G took that concept with him even though he grieved.

He tried to live by that concept, but it was tested on his thirteenth birthday when his stepmother ruined his party. She came into the venue drunk and outraged with hardcore evidence that her husband's sons were selling dope. She yanks G's brother Darius by the hair and yells in his face that he is ignorant like his father, and she leaves.

The boys never spoke to her again, but their little sister had no choice, that wasn't her stepmother, that was her biological mother. She forgave her mother, and she prayed that her brothers would too. Darius never forgave her till this day.

At sixteen years old, G was awarded a trophy for being the best football player in the state, and he was awarded the president award at his school. G thought back to when classes begin to get harder for him, and he found himself hating school. Low grades shows that education is no longer a top priority, so he got kicked off of the football team until he brought his grades up.

He never did. He settled for passing grades. G would sit in class and draw all day long. He would receive detention for sketching in class, but he called is designing. He would imagine himself watching gorgeous models walk the runway wearing his creative designs. G was passionate about style and wardrobe. He created a brand, and that's what he wanted to do. So he graduated from high school, and decided to take a break from school to focus on his craft and his identity.

G & G: LIVE WITH NO EDITS

G understood himself to be a passionate and driven young manthat strives to do the right thing every time. He's a by the book type of guy that takes great care of his family and the people that look out for him. G adores women, but he finds that they could be a distraction. So he limits his interactions with them, until a couple of months after his nineteenth birthday.

G meets this cute older girl at work. She's about yeh tall and this small. She's a cute little thing, she was just hood. She straight out of projects, and she makes sure everybody know it. Some kind of way, G thought she was the funniest and most intriguing character he ever encountered, and he started a sexual relationship with her. A few months later, his interest in her was fading away. She was no longer funny, she was lazy. She was not intriguing, she was entertaining for fifteen seconds.

Just as he picked up the phone to break it off with her, she was calling him to inform him that she just left the doctor, and she was pregnant with his baby. Now he's twenty, no job, finding out that his baby's mama is a crackhead, his grandmother could be dying from cancer, he got shot by the police, and he's in jail. He comes back to the present moment, and says a prayer that he doesn't age like Sanka in jail. He prays that God gets him out of here as soon as possible. Then he focuses on Sanka.

G : What did you do!?

Sanka : Possession of an unregistered gun, a lot of drugs, money, and being black in America. Mi was riding in mi brand new, 1978 Ford Mustang, Black Cobra, with red detailing, black interior, with the leather seats. Man mi had the windows down on the beautiful April day.

I was blasting the Commodores- Too Hot Ta Trot, through my speaker. I was on the way to deliver some heroin, then I was going to take a ride to the beach, blow some trees and ease mi mind. Life was great for me. I had been putting in hard work on the streets since I was 8 years, so by 20, I was set. I had stopped at a red light when a bloodclaat cop pulled up on the side of me.

G & G: LIVE WITH NO EDITS

He took one look at me, then at my car and hit me with the lights. I pulled over and the first thing he said to me was, "Aren't you too black to own a beauty like this?" Being the smart mouth I was, I quickly said, "Aren't you jealous? I guess being a bloodclaat cop doesn't come with too many benefits." He arrested me and I've been in here ever since.

G : You mean to tell me that it's been forty years. I know you have to be getting out soon, right?

Sanka : They sentenced me sixty years.

G : *shakes head* They love to see a black man in chains.

Sanka : What are you doing here?

G : My baby mama set me up. I walked in on her with a joint in her mouth, some cocaine and weed on the table and a glass of Ciroc in her hand.

Sanka: How did that lead you here?

G : She was eight months pregnant with my son. I yelled at her for a while, resulting in me taking all her drugs, and I left her house. She called the police and told them I hit her, and she told them about the drugs. Crooked behind cop shot me and broke my jaw because she told them that I hit her! He didn't like that .

Sanka : How long did they give you?

G : Five years. I didn't have too much drugs on me, but I'm going to miss a whole five years of my son's life. That is a very critical time for a father to be in his child's life. I really didn't have a father growing up. He was out serving drugs all day and all night.

When I went over to his house, he was only there to sleep and have sex with his wife. Then he got arrested when I was six. So I just wanted so much more for my boy. I need to have a real relationship with him. He needs to have someone he could trust and depend on at all times. He needs someone to teach him how to be a man. Living with his mama, all he is going to learn is how to be a junkie.

Sanka : You didn't know she was a junkie before you impregnated her?

G : I knew she smoked weed. I saw her sniff coke once before the pregnancy, but we made an agreement that that was the last time. I had been working a lot lately, trying to stack all the money I could so that when my boy got here, I could spend more time at home. Man, not knowing what she was doing. This is a disaster!.

Sanka : Everything is going to work out for you, Young King. As soon as your five years are up, you go straight home to your boy and never leave his side again.

G : I'm not sure everything is going to be okay. Now that I know she could care less about my baby, it might not be. Plus, I put all the money in a savings account that only she and I can access. She might go take that money and spend it on drugs *screams* God, help me!

Sanka : Do you have any siblings that could possibly step in as a father figure until you touchdown?

G : Yeah, but honestly, they aren't exactly the role model type. Don't get me wrong, I love my brothers, but they're just like my dad, serve drugs for a living and sex on anything with breast and a fat boonkey.

Sanka : Where did you work?

G : At a warehouse. My brothers didn't want me selling drugs. They started when they were eight and seven. I was six. My oldest brother said I was different from them. I had brains and talent. and he didn't want me in the streets.

Sanka : Six, seven, and eight. Did you have the same mother?

G : No. We all have different mamas, but my stepmother, Takiya, kept us close.

Flashback to 1998

Darnell Jr is five , Darius is four, and Keith is three.

Takiya : When am I going to be able to have your child, Darnell? You have me watching all your kids, but I can't have one of my own?

Darnell: I have too freaking many kids as it is, Takiya. I'm out here in these streets trying to provide for you and my boys, and it's not easy. Everywhere I go, I have to carry a gun and look over both shoulders for killers, robbers, and the police. Who knows when my last day on this earth is, because everybody is out to get me! I have the weight of the world on my shoulders and still manage to hold both of your hands. Please baby just stay down with me, and I promise one day I can stop hustling and give you all the time you deserve. *His beeper goes off.* But not right now. I have to catch this play. I'll see you when I get back! Go cook that bomb stuff you made last week, that I liked! I'll be back later on. (Pyummm) *runs out of the door*

Takiya: *release heavy sigh, goes to den with Darnell's three sons* Hey, boys! Are you hungry?

Darnell Jr: Yes. Where did my Daddy go? He said he was going to play cars with us.

Takiya: Your daddy had to go to work, but I'll play cars with you and then we can finish cooking. Come in the kitchen with me so you can get a snack first. *The three boys run to the kitchen*

Darnell Jr.: Taky, where does my Daddy work at? I know you sell houses, but what does my Daddy sell?

Taky: Oof, uhm Darnell sells uhm... mind escape games. It is very popular in the world, but we are not of the world. We are for God. So please don't ever mess around with the things that your daddy sells. It's not good for you. Okay, boys?

The boys stare at Taky with a look of confusion. They can't seem to understand that concept of working for income. So their main concern right now is who is going to be here watching, teaching, and raising me. They are well aware boys that wonder sometimes. Keith comes outraged that the thought and he screams.

Keith: Taky, I'm getting pretty tired of my daddy not being here when I get here. I love you, but dang! This is my Daddy's house, but I'm always here with you. When am I ever going to see my daddy? For real? This man magically always disappears when I search the house for him. I'm sick and tired of being abandoned by my own father. He knows that I exist, but I barely know what he looks like.

He releases a loud sigh. The house remains quiet for the next two hours. No one spoke a word after Keith's outburst. Takiya feels like she is being abandoned by Darnell, but she doesn't want to let go of the idea of being together with him. The reality that she truly is being abandoned by Darnell is blurry to her because she often thinks of the fantasy life once he does make her a priority.

Until then, I'm going to allow you to control and use me up. Ask whatever you want. Ask me to watch your kids. I'll say yes. Ask me to cook for you. I'll say yes. Ask me to wash your clothes, everyday. I'll say yes. Ask me to borrow some money. I'll say yes, because I'm waiting for the day you learn to appreciate me. And I'll be around just for that particular moment because I love you so much. That's a Godly trait, but everybody is not Godly people.

Takiya calls the boys to go get ready for a shower. She finishes up the dishes from cooking that bomb stuff that

Darnell likes so much. The kids enjoyed it too, but not with their daddy. Takyia walks to the bathroom to see the boys looking in the mirror, comparing their muscles.

Darnell Jr: Look, Taky! We're strong!

Takiya: I see! You have huge muscles! I'm scared of you guys!

Darius: Don't be afraid of us. We are going to use these muscles to protect you from the monsters!!

Takiya: *smiles hard* Thank you so much, Darius! I truly appreciate that.

Darius: Taky, I know Daddy is working, but how come he never eats with us? My friend at school Daddy eats with him every night.

Keith: My friend's daddy be picking him up from school. My Daddy doesn't ever pick me up from school.

Takiya: Because your daddy has to make money so that you can eat. And I will definitely tell him about picking you up from school, Keith.

Darnell Jr: But I'd rather starve with him than eat without him.

Keith says in a baby voice.

Keith: But I'd rather starve with him. Boy stop! You're tripping. I'm not starving if I don't have to, but I do want my Daddy to pick me up from school sometimes.

Takiya burst out into tears.

Takiya: I know what you mean, Darnell Jr.

Keith quickly understands that Darnell is the root of the problem. He has his brother sad and in pain. He's watching this woman cry, and she's not even related to him. That's when the hatred starts. Keith thinks that hating Darnell will hurt him, yet Keith is the only one going to face the consequences.

Keith: Don't cry, Taky. At least we're here with you. We got each other. We don't need him.

Takiya: * kisses Keith's forehead.* I don't think you should think like that, Keith. Come on y'all so we can read a story, and then you guys can go to sleep. It's getting late.

All of the boys have on their pajamas. Takiya reads *Are You My Mother* by Dr. Suess.

Darius: Taky, can I call you mama?

Takiya: * look surprised* Darius, you already have a mommy. I don't think she would like that very much.

Darius: But you treat me better than her. She doesn't read to me, or teach me, or even cook for me like you. I wish you were my mommy. I love you, Taky! *hugs her*

Takiya: * cries* I love you too, Darius! I love all three of you guys

All 4 of them are hugging.

The next day, Darius is back home at his Mama's house with her three other kids running around acting crazy. His mama is smoking weed with her homegirl in the living room.

G & G: LIVE WITH NO EDITS

Darius: Mama, I'm hungry.

Brionna: Go tell Brica to make you some noodles.

Darius: Mama, I want you to cook.

Brionna: Cook what? Lil boy you better get out my face.

Darius: Taky would have cooked.

Brionna: Do you think I care about what your lil play play stepmama would do for you? At least I'm feeding your lil ugly tail. Gone ni!

Darius: *cries* I wanna go live with Taky!

Brionna: That lady does not want you little crying baby! On the other hand, you can use my phone to call her. Matter of a fact, call your daddy. Tell him to come get your sickening behind and drop you right off to his little sadity housemaid. I have too many kids in this house anyway! *screams* All y'all need to just Shut up and leave me alone!! Brica take them kids outside, and here Darius. The phone is ringing.

Brionna dials Darnell's number and gives the phone to Darius.

Darius: Daddy! *walking out of the room* Can you come get me? I want to live with you. My mama is too mean.

Darnell: What do you mean too mean?

Darius: She won't do nothing but smoke stink cigarettes with Domo all day. She won't cook me nothing to eat. She calls me a sickening punk. I just wanna come live with you, Daddy! Please!

Darnell: I'm coming, Darius.

Fifteen minutes later

Darnell: * storms through the door, snatches Brionna by the arm and drags her in the room* What is wrong with you, Brionna? You must have forgotten who I am. Let me remind you. *back hand slap her until she falls to the ground* You have my baby calling me, BEGGING to leave his MAMA's house! I'm going to take you down to that court TOMORROW so you can take me off child support, and I'm taking my baby

38

with me. Make sure that your hair is done because I'm not taking you anywhere with me looking like that. You have let yourself go. You disgust me. *storms out her room, goes to Darius' room* Are you ready, little man?

Darius: Yes, Daddy.

Darnell: * slams the front door* Don't worry. You'll never have to come back here if you don't want to.

Darius: I don't! I hate this place, and I hate that woman! * gets in the front seat*

Darnell: Darius, you know Daddy works all the time and I don't know how Takiya would feel about me making you her responsibility full time.

Darius: Taky loves me, Daddy. She won't mind.

Darnell: We have to ask her, but until then, I'll take you to Mama Lee's house.

Darius: Can I please stay with you for now, Daddy? I'm tired of sitting up in the house. Then grandma is probably watching the stories! The only young and the restless I care about right now is me!

Darnell: *stares at Darius for awhile, until his l beeper goes off* Alright. *turns up radio with Ludacris Roll Out blasting through the speakers, and they take off. Fifteen minutes later, they pull up to the block. As soon as they get out of the car, Darius is greeted by Darnell's best friend, Tellie. They are both twenty-six years old.

Tellie: Wassup, lil bruh!

Darius: Wassup, Uncle Tellie *Tellie picks him up and flies him around*

Darnell is serving a feen on the corner

Tellie: How do you feel, Lil Man?

Darius: I'm okay.

Tellie: Do you want to talk about it?

Darius: I'm tired of my mommy not paying me any attention. She doesn't feed us. She sits around smoking those stinky cigarettes in the house all day long, and if I ask for something, she tells me to ask my sister. When I cry, she calls me a "sickening lil punk."

Tellie: * replies very sternly* Don't say punk anymore. Continue.

Darius: She just let my brother and sisters dirty up the house and doesn't clean up or even tell us to clean up. It all just hurt my feelings, and I don't like living there.

Tellie: I'm so sorry you have to go through that, Lil Darius. You're mama wasn't alway like. She used to be the finest thing on the block, and sweet as could be. We lost contact with her for a couple of years because her parents moved. Then next thing you know, she was back in the neighborhood. Even then, she kept on a fly outfit and her hair was always done.

    She looked like she had it all together. When your daddy finally stepped to her, she played hard to get so we definitely thought she was a "good girl" because your Daddy could pull anybody! I mean anybody. Your Daddy was the lady's manager. So, he started taking your mama out on lil dates, on shopping sprees, gave her money, all that.

Then one day, he wanted to go over to her house, but she was acting skeptical. She would come up with excuse after excuse. So your daddy thought she had another man. We actually followed her home.

Man, Darius, you won't believe this. We sat outside for three hours to see if a man or anybody for that matter would go in or come out. Just as the clock struck six pm, she came out of the house with three kids that didn't look like they had had a bath in weeks. Your brother's hair wasn't cut or the girls' hair wasn't done. They didn't have good clothes. Nothing.

Your daddy stepped out of the car and put the worst shocked expression on her face. She looked miserable that he found out what she was hiding. We found out those were all her kids, and they all have different daddies. He went inside the house and that also looked like it hadn't been cleaned in months.

He looked in all the closets. The kids didn't have any clothes or shoes. The fridge was empty, all that. Your daddy was livid! He couldn't believe what he had just seen. He couldn't understand how she could look so good all the time and not as much as get the kids haircut or braided.

She was blowing all the money on herself. She could care less about the kids. Your daddy left her, but a few months later, she pulled up on the block pregnant with you. Your daddy was devastated because he already knew how she treated her other kids, but that's why you are always with me, Taky, or Mama Lee. That rare occasion of you being over there helped you understand why you aren't over there.

Darius: I know she's my mama, but do I have to like her?

Tellie: Listen, don't hold a grudge against anyone. It's won't be good for your soul. Love, even if it's from a very far distance so you can keep your peace. You understand?

Darius: Yes sir. I wish Taky was my mommy. She always reads to us and plays with us. She even cooks all the time, and she keeps my daddy's house clean.

Tellie: Yeah, I respect Taky too. I think eventually your daddy is going to marry her. So she'll be your stepmama.

Darius: For real?

Tellie: I mean I don't know, but that's what he's telling me. Don't say anything to her about it.

Darius: I won't. Do you know where my brothers are? I think they might be hungry.

Tellie: *laughs loudly* Alright. Come on. Let's go pick them up, and I'll take y'all to Chuck E. Cheese to get you some pizza.

Darius: *jumps up quick* Yes! You're the best, Uncle Tellie!

Tellie: Darnell, come here. Let me holla at you right quick. The things that Darius is explaining to me are disturbing, and I wish you would take some time out to spend it with your son. He needs you man. Take care of your kids man. Do better. I'm about to take them to Chuck E. Cheese.

Later on that same day, Darnell and Takiya are in their bedroom.

Darnell: Takiya, we need to talk.

Takiya: What's wrong, baby?

Darnell: I had to go get Darius from his mama house today because she's been mistreating him, and he says he no longer wants to live with her. I told him he had to live with my mama, but he insists on living here. He wants you to be his new mommy.

Takiya: *smiles* I would love to!

Darnell: Dang, I didn't know you felt like that.

Takiya: Darnell, you do realize that every time those boys come over here, I am the one who feeds them, plays with them, and teaches them. Quite naturally, we created a bond. I love those boys as my own so I won't mind pretending to be his real mom because I already feel it in my heart.

Darnell: I love you, Takiya. You know that?

Takiya: Of course, Darnell.

Darnell: Baby, I'm serious. I swear when it's all over, and I don't have to trap anymore, I'm going to give you the world. Whatever your heart desires, you can have it. That's a promise. But right now, these people ain't paying enough to be a slave all day and night. They want us to dedicate all our time to their businesses, but they're the only ones profiting from it.

All you have enough money to do is pay your bills and all you have is enough time to sleep. That's not the lifestyle I'm striving for. I want to take trips whenever I feel like it, buy nice homes and cars. I wanna go to the mall and not worry about prices. I would like to fill my refrigerator up with groceries and still have money to put in a savings account for my sons to go to college.

Takiya: I would love to do all those things too baby, but your line of work is probably the most dangerous of them all. Everyday when you leave this house, I pray to God that the police don't lock your black tail up, or that someone doesn't shoot you dead. I pray you come home every night so your sons won't have to grow up without a father, but honestly Darnell, even though you aren't dead or in jail, your sons are still growing up without a father. You claim you're doing this for them, but they don't care about money right now.

Toys are all fun and games until you don't have anybody to play with. Kids remember who was there with them to play with the toys. They remember who put them on those nice clothes. They remember who fed them all that food in the refrigerator. You have to take time off for your kids, Darnell. Darnell Jr. told me, he would rather starve with you than to eat alone. Keith said all he wants is for his Daddy to pick him up from school sometime.

Darnell: *sigh* I understand, Takyia. You don't have to lay it on me so harshly. That's mean.

Takiya: Nobody is playing with you right now, Darnell. I'm giving you something to think about while you're out in those streets, while I'm here praying you make it home safely every night.

Master P and Mia X, Ghetto love begins to play.

Darnell: *pulls Takiya close enough to kiss her* As long as you keep praying, I'll keep coming home to your fine praying self every night. I love you, girl.

Takiya: I love you too, baby.

They stay up and make love all night long. Nine am the next morning, the doorbell rings. Takiya opens the door to Tellie bringing home the three boys.

Takiya: *smiling* Good morning.

3 boys: Taky!! * hugs her*

Tellie: Wassup, Takiya!

Takiya: Did y'all eat?

Tellie: Yeah, they should be good for the next couple hours. How are you doing?

Takiya: I'm doing good. How are you?

Tellie: I can't complain. Is Darnell awake?

3 boys: Daddy! Daddy! Daddy!

Takiya: He is now.

Tellie: *laughs* Right.

The three boys enter the room, and immediately jump on Darnell. Keith peels the cover off of his face and looks at his eyes. They looked puffy and dry.

3 boys: Daddy, wake up!!

Darnell: *sits up* I'm up. Good morning, little soldiers?

3 boys: Wassup, Daddy!

Darnell: Did you have fun with Uncle Tellie?

3 boys: Yes, Sir!!

Darnell Jr.: We went to Chuck E. Cheese, for an extremely long time, and we ate pizza and ice cream.

Darius: And Uncle Tellie took us to the mall and picked us out some super fly kicks. Come on y'all. Let's go get our shoes to show, Daddy!

Darnell gets up and walks to the bathroom. His beeper goes off while he is brushing his teeth. He calls someone.

Darnell: Wassup? Nah I'm chilling with my family today. Yeah. Ok. You just make sure y'all are on top of your game. We can't afford no slip ups. Y'all some grown men, and I'm not your daddy! But I am somebody's daddy, so handle yourselves accordingly because I will not be present today;

3 boys: Daddy, where are you at?

Darnell: I gotta go. Keep control! Don't let it control you!

Darnell Jr.: Daddy, look!

Keith: Mine are fresher than theirs.

Darnell: *laughs* They are all super fresh. What y'all wanna do today?

3 boys: Chuck E Cheese!

Darnell: Y'all just went to Chuck E. Cheese yesterday. How about we go to Flying Frogs, then we can go see the monster movie.

Keith: Monsters Inc!! *smiling hard*

Darnell Jr and Darius: *wide eyes* Yayy!

Darnell: Then we can go to the mall and get y'all some fresh, clean clothes to go with your super fresh, clean kicks. And then we are going to come back home to cook some shrimp pizza.

3 boys: Yayyy! *run* Taky!! Go get dressed! Daddy is about to take us to go have some fun!

Taky: I have to get you dressed first.

Darnell Jr.: Uh huuun. We are big boys. We can get ourselves dressed today, Taky!

Takyia: * laugh* Okay.

Once five year old Darnell Junior, four year old Darius, and three year old Keith are in their bedroom, Darnell Junior tries to take the lead, but Keith shows him who's the boss of him.

Darnell Jr.: Keith, what do you want to wear?

Keith: I'm going to pick out my own clothes. I don't need your help, but thank you.

Darius: I need some help, Darnell Jr. What am I supposed to wear?

Darnell Jr.: Go get some shoes from the closet then we are going find a shirt to match. *both boys go to the closet*

Darius: I want to wear these. These are too fresh.

Darnell Jr.: I'm going to wear these. And then, how about this shirt, and you can wear this shirt.

Darius: What about pants, Darnell Jr.?

Darnell Jr.: I'm going to wear these shorts and you are going to wear these ones.

Keith: *quietly dressing himself, looks in the mirror, admiring himself, looks at his brothers and burst out laughing* Y'all look country! That doesn't even match! Let me dress you. *grabs different outfits for his brothers and they put them on and look good* Now y'all look fresh like

me. Y'all gotta get some style if you gone be out in public
with me.

Darnell Jr.: Yeah. You're good!! Come on so we can show
Taky and Daddy.

Darius: Wait, hold up! We have to brush our hair! *grabs
brush, brushes his head, Darnell Jr's head, then Keith's.

Keith: Okay. Now we're ready!

3 boys: *run* Daddy, Taky, Daddy!

Darnell and Taky are in the room kissing when the boys run
in.

Keith: Yuck!

Darnell Jr.: That's what grown ups do when they love each
other.

Keith: I know, but it's still nasty.

Takyia: Ooooo y'all boys are too fresh!

Daddy: They even brushed their hair.

Takyia: *smiles* I see. Y'all look good. I'm proud of you.

Daddy: You think you're independent now?

Darnell Jr.: Yeah!

Darius: What does that mean, Darnell Jr.?

Darnell Jr.: It means that we can do things by ourselves.

Keith: We can't cook by ourselves.

Darnell: You better learn. Me and Alene had to do everything for ourselves when we were your age cause my mama always left us home alone. You need to get to a point where you don't need anybody for anything because you can't depend on nobody. Not even me. Nobody is going to do anything for you.

Keith: Are you going teach us how to cook?

Darnell: Yeah. Tonight when we come back home. Come on. Y'all ready?

Mary J. Blige - Family Affair

Everybody gets in Darnell's 1997 Lexus riding through the city of Savannah.

The kids are playing at Flying Frogs. Then everybody goes to the movies to watch Monster Inc. After the movie is over, they're in the mall shopping, Darnell doesn't put a price limit on anybody today. Whatever they want, he buys it. After that, they go across the street to Kroger to get the pizza ingredients.

Chef Londonaire at-home shrimp pizza ingredients:
2 lb medium peeled and deveined shrimp
Pillsbury pizza dough
Chef Londonaire's special pizza sauce
Kraft's triple cheese and Sargentos Colby Jack cheese
Chef Londonaire's choice of toppings: Bell pepper, onion, mushrooms, cubed yellow squash, thyme, rosemary, and basil

The Family pulls back up to the house around seven that night.
Darnell: Come on y'all boys.

Darnell Jr.: Wake up, Keith! We are about to make pizza!

Everyone walks in the house.

Takyia: Everybody wash your hands before touching anything!

3 boys: Yes ma'am.

Darnell's beeper goes off with an urgent message. He quickly calls the number.

Darnell: WHAT!!? JUST NOW? I'M ON MY WAY! Takiya, I'm sorry! Juju just got shot 5 times. Please stay in the house with the kids. I gotta go to the hospital.

Takyia: Oh my gosh! Please be safe, and don't do anything stupid.

Darnell: *runs out the house and hops in his Lexus, no music* Ion know why these boys insist on messing with my crew, but it's gone stop tonight! Soon as I leave this hospital, it's on! Believe that. If my boy dies. I'm killing everybody. I'm blowing up their whole hood!

G & G: LIVE WITH NO EDITS

silence

Ten minutes later, Darnell swerves into the hospital's parking lot, at the same time as Tellie, Quel, Torrance, and Mel. They're in the same car.

Darnell: What happened?

Quel: We were all in the house, getting ready to go back out on the block. Juju walked out the door first and as soon as this man stepped out, bullets went flying. When bruh fell, the bullets stopped, and we ran outside.

Tellie: I bust their tires so they couldn't even go anywhere.

Torrance: Man, I had came out of the house with the rocket launcher, and blew up the whole freaking car!

Tellie: That man Ty came and brought Juju up here. All us had grabbed everything out the house and dipped before the police popped up.

Darnell: SHOOT! So y'all don't even know who it was?

Tellie: Nah. The shooters are probably still burning up as we speak. You know it takes fifty years for the police to come to the hood.

Darnell: We'll find out real soon. Those boys were waiting for all of us probably.

Quel: Yeah they were waiting! I'm talking about as soon as this man opened the door, bullets went flying.

Mel: Come on. y'all. Let's see what the doctors are talking about.

They all walk into the hospital and see their other friend.

Mel: There goes Ty!

Ty: He's in surgery right now.

The doctor comes walking toward them.

Doctor: He lost a lot of blood. Would any of you be willing to donate blood?

Torrance: You ain't even gotta ask all that. It's just the matter of who has the same blood type. I'm Type O.

Doctor: So is he. So...

Torrance: Well let's go! Ain't no time to waste!

Eight hours later, Mel, Quel, Tellie, Darnell, Ty, Juju's mama and sister are all in the waiting room.

Doctor: Hello, Family.

Mama: * jumps up* Is my baby okay?

Doctor: Oh he's doing just fine. He has a broken jaw, his left shin bone is shattered, he has two broken ribs on his right side, but dear God, he's alive. He's in a whole lot of pain right now but he is conscious, sort of. He's doped up on a lot of pain medication.

Sister: Can we see him?

Doctor: Of course. Two at a time though. Mama and sister take off running.

G & G: LIVE WITH NO EDITS

Doctor: *yelling* Room 246!

Tellie: How's Torrance?

Doctor: Oh he's fine. He's asleep right now. Giving blood will definitely wear you out. But as long as he gets the proper rest, he'll be back to normal in 72 hours. We took a lot of blood.

Quel: Thank you so much Doc! We truly appreciate your hard work!

Doctor: Oh it's my pleasure. It's just a shame how many gun violence victims fill up this place everyday. I can't wait til it comes to an end.

Everybody: Me too. *shakes heads*

Doctor: Your friend will be okay though. Just keep your heads up.

61

Business Major: One Month Later

Mel, Torrance, Quel, Darnell, Tellie, Ty, and Juju who is sitting in a wheelchair, are posted on the block. Mel and Torrance are serving feens, Quel is counting money, Darnell and Tellie are laughing at a junkie dancing.

Tellie: Boy you need to be on America's Got Talent! You sure are working those legs.

Darnell: *dying laughing*

Juju: I heard he can sing too.

Darnell: You can sing, Sho You Right?

Sho You Right: Yeah! SHO CAN!

Juju: Let us hear something, Sho You Right. *looks at Tellie* That boy got talent.

Sho You Right: *sings vocals* up the scale, all the way to soprano, to alto, all the way down to tender, and end with a note higher than Mariah Carey's capability

Tellie: Damn, Sho You Right! You sure did just blow.

Quel: How did you get hooked on these drugs?

Sho You Right: I was smoking weed with some men from round the way. Come to find out, it was more than weed in the blunt.

Tellie: Shoot. I really hate that happened to you, man.

Sho You Right: Yeah, me too, but it's like I just can't stop. I go crazy without it. My family disowned me, and I have no one to turn to but drugs.

Juju: Man the streets ain't no place for you. You still have a good mind.

Tellie: Yeah man. Have you ever tried to stop?

Sho You Right: Yeah, but then I start tweaking and lose all my will power. I'm not disciplined.

Tellie: I tell you what. If you promise me to work hard on your singing and dancing, I'll pay for you to go to the best rehab in the city, for as long as it takes you to get clean and never want to touch a drug again.

Sho You Right: You mean that?

Tellie: I'm serious as your ability to sing. So what do you say?

Sho You Right: I promise, man. I swear I promise! *smiling*

Tellie: Come on, get in the car. We are going to leave right now.

Sho You Right: Can we get something to eat first? *still smiling, walking to the car*

Tellie: Man I'll take you anywhere you want to go.

Sho You Right: I want some Salt Water Grill. Those hush puppies are to live for.

Tellie: You're on to something, Sho You Right. *shuts car door*

Juju: That boy Tellie has a good heart.

Mel: Yes it is!

Torrance: Most times, I consider quitting this shift. It's corrupting our people, but it's the only way I know how to get money. It's the only source of income that'll support the lifestyle I want to live.

Ty: You right, Torrance. This is corrupting our people, our neighborhood, the black community as a whole. I've been thinking about starting my own business.

Darnell: What kind of business?

Ty: I don't know yet. I just want out of the game. I know if I start now, I'll be straight in a year. I'm willing to stay down until I come up.

Torrance: I always wanted my own lawn care service.

Ty: Yes, Torrance! You're on to something! But you know what? We need to invest some of this money into a decent education, so nobody can bamboozle us.

Torrance: My lady goes to Savannah State right now. She says that the students teach themselves. What we can do is buy some of those books and just read up on how to be business smart.

Ty: I'm saying, don't talk about it, if you aren't really bout it.

Torrance: Boy I got money stacked! I can bust a move right now!

Ty: Well this is what we are going to do. We can go to State, figure out what books the business major students are reading, go to the bookstore, buy em.

Torrance: Yeah. Then let's go to Home Depot, go half on the equipment.

Ty: Yeah, But Torrance we have to be super legitimate and go half on a truck and trailer.

Torrance: Come on, Ty man, I'm down.

Ty: Alright Torrance. Let's get it then.

Torrance: Fasho! *dap everybody up* Aye, we are about to bounce. I'll holla at y'all boys tomorrow. Y'all be safe out here.

Ty: *daps everybody* For real. Y'all boys be safe.

Mel, Juju, Darnell, and Quel are the only ones left on the block.

Mel: A man like me is not with the school jive.

Darnell: Boy me either. I couldn't even stand being in high school. The teachers used to blow my whole day.

Quel: You ain't lying boy. In the tenth grade, I remember Ms. Brown said just like this, "Boy your black tail ain't gone never amount to anything!" Man I told that old white hoe to kiss my behind, and I never went back to school.

Darnell: Man then school teachers don't care nothing bout us. They ain't making no money so they ain't gone teach us to be smarter than them cause they don't wanna see us pass them.

Mel: That sound bout right too, Darnell.

Darnell: I mean think about it. They are getting paid what, less than five thousand a month to sit up in the jailhouse with them seeds of Chucky for 7–8 hours a day. Of course they wanna see us down, misery loves company. That much is going to cover your bills, clothes, and food.

Juju: They need to increase the teachers' pay rate, at least times two. They're watching some of those students come out to be doctors and lawyers, but they're the ones teaching them how to be doctors and lawyers. Then what about the athletes? Some of them could care less about what the teacher was talking about. As long as he can throw a football a hundred yards, he graduates and goes pro. Now he's touching more money than she can make in her entire career.

Mel: Dang Juju. You sound like a scholar boy. *Darnell and Quel laughing*

Juju: That jive ain't even funny boy. My mama was a teacher. Then when she got done babysitting them jungle animals, she had to go to another job, just to provide for me and my sister, and we barely even got to see her.

Darnell: Ain't it boy, I ain't never seen my mama. She was always at work.

Juju: That's what I'm saying. Parents are being separated from their children and the kids are left to raise themselves. They don't have anybody to turn to but the men in the streets who are really getting money. They are standing on the block all day, it's easy to access them. Shoot, us. We be out here all day watching the kids play in these streets.

Darnell: Aint it. My mama's boyfriend was a drug dealer, that taught me everything I know.

Quel walks off to serve someone in an unmarked car.

Undercover cop: Aye man. How much for a pop? I'm tweaking like a mug.

Quel: Hundred a pop.

Ucc: Money good. *Pulls out a stack* Let me get 5 of em.

Quel: *goes to hand him the drugs, the cop handcuffs him and other cops jump out the cut. They run but the cops tackle them and handcuff them. Juju, who is in a wheelchair, is trying to roll out, but the cop catches him and searches him.

Juju: I don't have anything man!

Cop: Yeah. I bet you don't.

Juju: Man, just leave me alone. I'm not bothering anybody.

Cop: You're bothering me. Making all that money. But you don't serve no purpose anyhow. *dying laughing* You're held captive to that wheelchair.

Juju: Man what's your purpose? The police ain't nothing but a big gang that just kills and arrests brothers for being black. The other cops are pulling off with Mel, Quel, and Darnell. Only one officer and Juju are left.

Cop: Yeah, you ain't none of my brother.

Juju: Yeah thank God for that.

Cop: Speaking of him. I hope you said your prayers recently cause you're surely about to go meet him.

Juju: Boy don't put nothing like...

Cop: *shoots Juju in the head* He talked too much. I don't know why he didn't die the first time. *lights cigarette, laughing as he walks to the car*

A week later, the next day after Darnell's court day, Takyia takes the three boys to see Darnell in jail.

Darnell: *sitting behind glass, holding the phone*

Takyia and the three boys are searching for Darnell.

Darnell Jr.: *screams when he sees him.*

Darius: Let me talk first.

Darnell Jr.: I'm the oldest. Let me talk first. *grab the phone* Hey, Daddy!

Darnell: Wassup, boy! Are you being good?

Darnell Jr.: Yes, Daddy. When is the police gonna let you come home?

Darnell: They gave me a whole year.

Darnell Jr.: *screams* A year!!? *Looks at everybody else with their shocked expressions.*

Darnell: Yeah man, but ima make sure you have the best birthday party cause you're about to be six years old! You're a big boy now.

Darius: Let me talk to Daddy now, Darnell Jr. *snatch phone* Hey, Daddy!

Darnell: Wassup, boy! I sure do miss you.

Darius: I miss you too, Daddy, but Taky has been holding down our fort, so we're okay.

Darnell: I'm glad to hear that! You talked to your mama?

Darius: No. She knows where I'm at, and she ain't come to see me. So I'm not going to see her.

Darnell: If that's how you feel, so be it.

Darius: Taky is my mommy now.

Darnell: I'm so glad you like Taky.

Darius: I don't just like her, I love her.

Darnell: Me too. You think I should make her my wife?

Darius: Yeah!

Darnell: Okay, but promise me you won't say anything.

Darius: I promise!

Darnell: Good. Let me talk to Keith.

Keith: *Unethusticastically* Wassup, Daddy.

Darnell: Wassup, Lil man. How are you doing?

Keith: Good.

Darnell: How are your mama and grandma doing?

Keith: Good.

Darnell: You being good?

Keith: Yes, Sir.

Darnell: I miss you, little man.

Keith: Okay. Taky wants to talk to you.

Darnell: *looks surprised and confused as Takiya is taking the phone* I hope you treat me better than Keith.

Takiya: *just stares*

Darnell: What's the matter, baby?

Takyia: Darnell... *heavy sigh* Juju was murdered the same day y'all got arrested.

Darnell: WHAT!?

Takyia: They say nobody saw anything. They found him with a bullet in the middle of his head around four o'clock.

Darnell: That was the same time we got arrested! You sure ain't nobody seen nothing?

Takyia: No. The little twelve year old boy found him in his chair, facing the house with a bullet in his forehead at four o'clock. He ran home and his people called the police. They say they don't have any type of evidence to build a case.

Darnell: What do you mean!!? The police did that, Takyia! I know for a fact! It's too obvious! He got killed right at the same time of our arrest and the police are saying that they are not even going to try to look for the killer. They did that! I know for a fact one of them weak crackers killed my dawg! * Crying hysterically*

Darnell Jr.: What's wrong with Daddy?

Takyia: Daddy's friend was murdered .

Darius: That means he's dead?

Takyia: *nods head*

Darius: Let me talk to him. Daddy. I know you are sad. They got you locked away like a zoo animal and your friend was murdered, but just try to keep your head up. Remember that all of us love you. Remember your boys are always gone hold it down for you, Daddy.

Darnell: Thank you, Darius. I truly appreciate that.

Guard: Your time is up.

Darnell: I love you, son. Let me talk to Taky real fast. Baby please take good care of my sons. Please make sure Darnell Jr. has the best birthday party a six year old could ask for. And please be safe.

Takiya : I got you, Baby.

Guard: It's time to go!

Darnell: I love you.

Takyia: I love you more.

Blue 4 Door: Two months later

Today is Darnell Jr.'s sixth birthday party. Brenda and Takiya have been together all week preparing for his party. They picked out his outfit, purchased the decorations, the cake, and sent out the invitation together. Mama Lee is having the party at her house, and she is cooking all of the food.

Brenda: Takyia, I just want to thank you for all that you do for my son and his brothers. Darnell Jr. comes home raving about you every time.

Takyia: It's really not a problem at all. I love those boys with a passion.

Keyawana, Keith's mother and Keith walk into the backyard and up to Brenda and Takyia.

Keyawana: Hey y'all!

Brenda: Hey, Keyawana! How are you feeling?

Keyawana: Excellent! How are you?

Takyia: Hey, girl! Hey, Keith!

Keyawanna: Hey, Taky!

Keith: Hey, Taky! *hugs her* Where are my brothers at?

Takyia: I think they're in the bouncy house.

Keith: Thank you for my brother, Ms. Brenda!

Keith takes off running.

Brenda: You're welcome, baby. He's so sweet.

Takyia: Yes it is.

Keyawana: All he talks about is Taky. Woman, you are a true blessing to those boys. Thank you so much.

Takyia: *smiling real hard* Thank you, Keya. It's not a problem at all. But you know what I notice? I don't think Keith likes Darnell, like at all.

Keyawanna: Girl I've been trying to get that out of him. Anytime I ask him about Darnell, he doesn't have two words to say. And I can't blame the poor baby. It's my fault. I didn't even know Darnell when I conceived my baby. Darnell was a one night thing that I regretted til the birth of my son.

I was dating another guy since middle school. He was charming, amazing, attractive, and everything you could dream of in a man. It went south after my twenty-first birthday. We moved in together and it didn't go well at all.

He started nagging about little pity stuff. He stopped communicating his feelings like he used to. He would stay

74

out on the couch all night. He would even go to sleep in the bed, I would wake up in the middle of the night, and he's gone back to the couch.

I thought he was seeing someone else, but I couldn't prove it. I went through his phone, call log, text messages, photos, but nothing. Something was off with him. I could feel it. One night we got into a shouting match, and I packed my bags and left.

I met Darnell at the club, and slept with him that night. Larry called me a couple of times but of course I was occupied. Three months later, I found out I was pregnant and I knew who the father was because I hadn't had sex with Larry in a month.

Takyia: Whoa.

Brenda: Exactly! Whoa. So your telling me that you don't know anything about Darnell? Because I know he wasn't there for you after you told him you were pregnant.

Keyawanna: Well, life got real hard after the pregnancy was revealed to everyone. Darnell was invited to the birth, but he didn't come. My mama's car broke down right there in the parking lot. So I called Darnell to see if he would come pick us up from the hospital.

This man sent his cousin to come get us. I was grateful for the ride, but he showed our son signs of abandonment since day one. There was nothing else to say. He came to see him two weeks later talking about, "whose white baby is this?" I could have killed him. And I never heard from Larry again.

Brenda: You met him at twenty-three, post Brenda. I drove that negro crazy! Me and my mama!!!!!

The two women burst out laughing.

Keyawanna: I didn't even have the energy to dial his number, but thank God for Mama Lee.

Brenda: She is an angel sent from heaven. She tried everything to make Darnell a good person. He turned out this way on his own. She didn't have much family to guide her either, but she knew she could get further in life at least by being nice.

Takyia: I truly hope this jail time will teach him a lesson when it comes to being present in these kids' lives. These kids are going to grow up hating him if he doesn't get his act together.

Everybody shakes their heads, when Tellie walks up.

Tellie: Hey, everybody!

3 women: Hey, Tellie!!!

Tellie: How y'all doing today?

3 women: Good.

Tellie: Takyia, Darnell said he was trying to call you today.

Takyia: Yeah. I've been so busy setting up, I kept missing the call. I'll reach him eventually.

Brenda: Yeah, the time is flying! Tellie, when are you going to have some kids?

Tellie: I don't want to bring any kids in this world knowing I'm not willing to sacrifice the time it will take to get my life in order before they're born. I'm not trying to play catch up after they are here. I would like to position myself to be as financially free as I possibly can so that I can provide my children with the best opportunities life could offer them

Brenda: Wow. How is Darnell surrounded by all of these smart people, yet he's acting incapable of growth.

Tellie: Aww. Y'all know how he is. He thinks he knows everything that he needs to know. He'll get his act together eventually. Hopefully, by the time it's too late.

A little boy runs toward the moon bounce with a hot dog. Mama Lee, Darnell's mama, walks up, speaks to Tellie, and tells the girls that the food is ready. They walk to the kitchen.

Darnell Jr.: Grandma! Where is the food? Hey, Uncle Tellie!

Tellie: Wassup, D! Happy birthday!

Darnell Jr.: Thank you!

Ms. Lee: Your mama is getting your plate right now. Go sit at the big table please.

Darnell Jr.: Yes ma'am.

Keith: *runs up with Darius* Hey, Grandma!

Darius: Hey, Uncle Tellie!

Mama Lee: Hey, my sweet baby *kiss his cheek*

Tellie: Wassup, little men! Are you guys having fun?

Keith and Darius hug him.

Darius and Keith: Yes sir!

Mama Lee: You guys go take a seat at the big table.

Darius and Keith: Yes, Ma'am!

Keith: You know that's the table that Grandma tells everybody about her business. I think I want to tell mine. Come on!

The boys are seated at the kids table as Torrance and Ty walk up and speak to the boys. Mama Lee invites Tellie inside to get some food.

Mama Lee: Come on in here, Tellie and fix you a plate.

Tellie smiles as he walks past Darnell Jr. Keith, Darius, Darnell Jr's five year old cousin, DJ.

Keith: We are gathered here together to celebrate my brother's birthday. You think we can get a round of applause for my big brother everybody?

They take a second to celebrate Darnell Jr. and it makes him feel very special. He's smiling so much, and it's just pure joy.

Keith: But on a serious level, I need to tell y'all something that's really bothering me.

Darnell Jr: What is it, Keith?

Keith: I really hate, Daddy. And I know it sounds weird to y'all because you adore that man, but I don't know that man. And I'm angry about it. I can tell you what every single last one of my classmates' dads look like. It was just the other day when I got to see my own dad's eyes up close.

Darius: That's deep. I got all this hatred towards my mom, I never noticed that I was being neglected by my father.

Keith: That's because he wasn't around enough to mistreat you like your mom.

Darnell Jr: Dad will be home in a years, and when he does, it'll be more days like that one when we went shopping and had fun.

Keith: I pray it all works out for you like that, but I've given up hope to build any relationship with the man. He keeps disappearing, and it is not cool. I'm over it.

Darius: I'm down for Daddy. I think he'll come home, and do the right thing. I want him to spend more time with us. We deserve that.

Darnell Jr: He will, Keith. I promise.

Keith: You can't make Daddy's promises for him. He'll have to prove that on his own.

Darnell Jr: You've been showing that you felt like this a long time ago. I'm glad you finally said something.

Keith: I had to. You guys, as my brothers, are the only people that understand. So I can't hold anything from you.

Darius: I promise to keep this a safe place.

Darnell Jr: I promise too, but I think you should like that hatred go, and forgive. You don't have to have a relationship to forgive him for your heart.

Keith: I think I could do that.

On the other side of the backyard, the grown folks have found their tribe, and the part is about to be on! The kids have their food. The parents can rest. The deck is shuffled, and the cards are on the table.

Ty and Torrance inform the crew that they're landscaping business is in full effect. They are seeing the client list get longer and longer. Keyawanna commits to being on the client list, and the guys are very appreciative. All of a sudden a lady is screaming in the background

Brionna: Oh I know I was invited to the party.

Tellie: Oh, Lord!

Takiya: Who is that?

Ty: Brionna, Darius mama.

Brionna: Well hey, Son! Long time no see. You don't care about your mama no more? Happy birthday, Lil Darnell. You look just like your daddy!

Tellie: Come on Brionna, man. Ain't nobody invited you to the party.

Brionna: And I wanna know why not!

Tellie: Look how you come around here acting!

Mama Lee: You are not welcomed round here. Gone and leave.

Brionna: I'm welcomed wherever my son is.

Mama Lee: You don't care nothing bout this here child.

Brionna: Whatever Mary Lee! I came for the imposter that's pretending to be MY son's mother! What's the fake's name? *looks at Domo*

Domo: Taky! *dying laughing*

Brionna: The heck is a Taky! Where you at imposter! *close eyes* 7, 8, 9, 10, ready or not, here I come!

Tellie: Gone with that childish jive, Brionna.

Brionna: That must be her right there cause I know the other two hoes!

Darnell Jr.: My mama not no hoe!

Keith is mugging Brionna hard.

Brionna: Shut yo big head up!

She mushes his head. Mama Lee grabs the boys and takes them in the house. Brenda runs up on Brionna and starts fighting.

Ty: Come on, y'all! It's kids out here.

Torrance grabs Brenda off Brionna. Tellie is holding Domo and Ty is carrying Brionna. They take them to the car, as Brionna is screaming for Ty to put her down.

Domo: You ain't gotta put me down. You're finer than chocolate!

Tellie: Shut up. Y'all stay the heck from around here.

Brionna: Oh. We'll leave, but this won't be the last you see of me, Tellie. Believe that!

Tellie and Ty go back to the party.

Torrance: I'm so sorry they messed up your party, Lil Darnell.

Darnell Jr.: My party is not messed up. My mama tore her up like John Cena!

Mama Lee: Come on, baby. Let's sing happy birthday.

Brenda is lighting the candles then everybody starts singing happy birthday. Tellie, Ty, and Torrance walk off. The women are passing out cake when the three men come back with three luxury toy cars.

Tellie: Happy birthday, Darnell Jr.!

Darnell Jr. turns around, screams, drop his cake, and runs to Tellie.

Ty: Here Darius and Keith. Darnell couldn't be the only one riding clean!

Darius sits his cake on the table and runs. Keith stuffs the whole cake in his mouth then runs.

Ty: Tellie brought these.

The three boys hops out of the cars to thank their uncle, Tellie.

Torrance: This one is from Uncle Ty and this one is from me.

Darnell Jr. empties the bags to see Ty brought three big super Nerf Guns. Torrance brought a Nintendo game system. The three boys are smiling as they're thanking the men. Takiya walks up and passes the phone to Darnell Jr.,

Takiya: Your daddy wants to talk to you.

Darnell Jr.: *grabs the phone* Hey, Daddy! Yeah!

Darnell Jr.: We are having the best fun in the world. Uncle Tellie got me and my brothers cars like y'alls! And Uncle Ty got us some super big guns. And Uncle Torrance got us a Nintendo!

Darnell: Is that so?

Darnell Jr.: Yes, sir! I wish you were here though, Daddy. Guess what, Daddy! Darius mama came to my birthday party screaming and acting crazy. Then she pushed my head and my mama beat her up, and Uncle Ty picked her up and carried her and her friend outta here! Yeah, she sho did! Here, Mama! Daddy wants to talk to you.

Brenda: Hello?

Darnell: Really, Brenda?

Brenda: Yes! She came out here all loud and showing her ignorance. All I know is I saw her mush my baby's head, and I transformed into the Incredible Hulk and Flash all at the same time until Torrance and Ty broke it up.

Darnell: If you see her again, please leave her alone because Ty and them aren't always going to be around.

Brenda: I'm thinking about that girl, long as she keeps her hands off my child. We don't have any problems.

Darnell: I'm warning you, Brenda. That girl is crazy.

Brenda: Okay!? And I'm crazy too! I dare her to try me again. You know what? Bye, Darnell, please. Here. *she says as she hands Takyia the phone. Takyia walks off.* Y'all go ahead and play before it gets dark out here.

Brionna and Domo are stakingout, down the block, waiting on Takyia when everybody comes out to their cars saying goodbyes.

Domo: Looks like the kids are going with her.

Brionna: It's all good. We are still going to follow her to see where they stay at. I got something for Barbie.

Domo: Oh shoot! All of the kids are getting in Keyawanna's car.

Brionna: *devious smile* Great! Plan activated! Let's go!

They pull the seats all the way back. She turns on the car lights and follows Takiya. Crime Affiliates' Crime Pays is playing in the background. Brionna drives onto Truman Parkway and pulls up to the side of Takyia's car. Domo crawls to the back seat, puts on a black ski mask, rolls down the window, pulls the gun up and out the window, and bust both of Takiya's right tires. Brionna speeds off fast. Takiya's car spins out of control, flips a couple times, then the car is leaking gas.

Ty and Torrance are getting on Truman, listening to UGK Gravy.

Torrance: I know for sure that Brenda was going to beat the brakes off Brionna had we not broken up that fight!

Ty: Word! Hold up! *turns down the radio* You smell that? *pulling closer to the crime scene*

Torrance: Oh shoot! Look at that! *drives closer*

Ty: I KNOW that ain't Darnell's Lexus!

Torrance: Damn it! Brionna's jealous self! *pulls over* Lord please don't let this girl be dead.

They run over to the car. Ty calls the police while they both are running to the driver side to find Takyia stuck.

Ty: We have to get you out of here before this car blows up! But you're going to have to help me.

Ty: They are on the way! *police sirens* Darn that was quick!

Torrance: This isn't the hood.

Ty: That gas is leaking rapidly! That's probably what you were smelling earlier.

Torrance: Please, Takyia! Help me get you outta here!

He pulls Takyia out as she's screaming. Ty turns and runs in the opposite direction, Torrance picks her up and runs as the car explodes. The ambulance pulls up with a stretcher.

Police: What happened?

Torrance: We found her like this!

Ty: Please do everything you can to save her! Ty's phone rings and it's Brenda calling* Hello?

Brenda: Hey, Ty. I was calling to see if y'all wanted to go out to get a drink. I tried to call Takiya to see if she wanted to go too, but she didn't answer. She must be never turned her ringer back on.

Ty: Brenda, Takyia just got in an exploding car accident.

Brenda: What! Did she survive? Where was the accident ?

Ty: She's alive, but she's in bad shape. We are not too sure as to what happened cause she's the only car involved. We're on the Truman between the Montgomery crosses and Eisenhower exit.

Torrance: Before the car blew up, it looked like two of the tires were flat.

Ty: Torrance just said she had two flat tires.

Brenda: Two flats!? That doesn't make any sense to me!

Police: There are bullet shells a few feet away from the car. Looks like this was an attempted murder.

Ty and Torrance's jaws drop as they look at each other.

Brenda: Attempted murder? That got darn Brionna!

They get to the hospital to see Takiya lying with closed eyes. Brenda, Keyawanna, the three boys, Takiya's mama, Harmon and sister and Ty and Torrance are all there. Two detectives walk in.

Detective Ryan: Good evening, everyone. My name is Detective Ryan, and this is my partner Detective Bell.

Bell: Hello. Is she conscious?

Harmon: Yes, but she just got out of surgery so she needs to get some rest.

Ryan: That is understandable, but we need to know if she saw anything before the accident, so we can go ahead and solve this case.

Harmonr: *nods her head* Takiya, honey, wake up. Detectives are here to speak with you.

Bell: Good evening, Takyia. I'm truly sorry about what happened to you.

Takyia: I'm just blessed to be alive.

Bell: Glad to hear you're in good spirits. Is there anything you can recall before the accident? Any cars trailing you?

Takyia: The last thing I saw was a blue, four-door car in my rear view with the bright lights on. Then next thing you know, I heard a gunshot and my back tire went flat then my front tire. Then the blue car sped off as my car spun out of my control, flipped a few times, then it caught a large fire.

Darius: My mommy has a blue car with four doors.

everybody looks at him

Bell: Did you have any enemies?

Brenda: Sir, excuse me. I don't think any more questions are necessary. We know exactly who did this.

Less than an hour later, cops are dragging Domo and Brionna out of Brionna's house in handcuffs. One cop comes out with Domo's gun in a plastic bag and a big bag of weed. Another officer has Brionna's two daughters and her son with him.

That Painful Feeling: Ten Months Later

Darnell is being released from prison. Tellie is picking him up. They are both smiling joyously, hug one another, then get in the car.

Tellie: Glad to have you back home, Darnell!

Darnell: I'm a free man! Good to see you man! What's the move?

Tellie: First, we are going to go to your mama's house.

Darnell: Oh no. I hope she doesn't come at me with any religion at all.

Tellie: If you ask me, Jesus is the reason you're out of this mess. You need to tighten up Darnell. I'm your boy, I wouldn't be if I was scared to tell you how I feel about your actions. Take into account that your sons' lives depend on you! You are the glue to that relationship. Keith out here disrespecting your name.

Darnell: What do you mean?

Tellie: You obviously had the wrong impression of yourself the other day. At the birthday party, Keith was telling his brothers how he lost all hope to reconcile his relationship with you. Darnell and Darius were totally down for you, but Keith says that he doesn't even know what you look like. That's just sad, Darnell.

Darnell: Come on, Tellie. Don't come at me with that sad jive today. I'm in a good mood today. I learned my lesson. Ima just be with my kids, and all you too take me to Kay's Jewelers because I'm about to propose to Takiya.

Tellie: Yes! I already knew that though. I told Darius that day I picked him up from crazy crazy's house for good.

Darnell: Yeah and I told him when Takyia brought him to see me right after I got locked up. She truly is a queen. And deserves to be treated like one.

Tellie: Well that is just beautiful. After that accident, I stopped by the grocery store to pick up Takiya some flowers. That's when I met a wonderful young lady. We've been dating since.

Darnell: That's what's up, Tellie. It's about to we get some good women in our lives.

Tellie: Yeah man. It's about time we grow up, and be good men for these good women. I'm leaving the game, Darnell. I don't want to sell drugs anymore.

Darnell: What!?

Tellie: No. The weight is too heavy for me now. It doesn't feel right to me anymore. I'm about to start my own record label.

Darnell: What?!

Tellie: Yeah, man. *smiling* Sho You Right has completely recovered, and with his talent, all he needs is the right type of exposure. I know he's going to have a successful career, and I know this young guy from out of Carver Village that goes by Smitty. He has the hottest rhymes I've heard in a long time. So I'm going for it. I don't have the tell, but I know how to recruit talent from a business standpoint.

Darnell: Alright then, Tellie! That's great!

Tellie: Yeah. I will move to Atlanta next month.

Darnell: Next month!?

Tellie: Yeah. I found a super nice spot for a reasonable price in Clayton County. It's not too far from downtown and plus you remember Brian from Woodsville?

Darnell: Yeah.

Tellie: He is a big time Dj up there now. So he knows all the hot spots and where everybody is. So I feel like everything is right. It's my time.

Darnell: That's what's up, Tellie! I'm really proud of you!

Tellie: Thank you, man. I think it's about time you get out the streets too, my friend.

Darnell: Man all I know is the streets.

Tellie: Then help me with the record label. You and the family move to Atlanta with me, man. I need you.

Darnell: Nah, man. Atlanta is too wicked for me.

Tellie: Wicked? It's wicked everywhere. So what?

Darnell: I don't want to leave Savannah.

Tellie: Fine.

Darnell: You remember T-note, from G street? He got caught snitching!

Tellie: Yeah. I heard about that. You remember big mouth Quincy? He's connected to the feds now. So he he's getting insider information, and he told me that the other day.

Darnell: Yep. Kyrie said both of them robbed somebody and T-note told the people that he didn't want no part, but Kyrie put a gun to his head and forced him to go.

Tellie: The crazy part is, I remember when they use to run on the playground together.

Darnell: That's what he said, they grew up tight like that. Boy that's some wicked jive dey. I couldn't do that to my friends.

They pull to Mama Lee's house. They get out of the car, and walk to the door. Darnell rings the doorbell . She takes a long time to open the door.

Darnell: What is taking so long?

Door slowly creeps open. Its pitch black inside. Darnell pulls Tellie's gun from his waist and kick in the door Mama!! *lights turn on and everybody screams surprise* Boy y'all almost got shot! Wassup, y'all!!!

3 boys: Daddy!!!

Darnell: There go my boys! Daddy missed y'all.

3 boys: We missed you too, Daddy!

Mama Lee: Hey, my baby!

Darnell: Hey, Mama!

Mama Lee: Well you know your mama made all your favorites because I know what they were feeding you, was causing malnutrition.

Darnell: You don't know the half *shakes head*

Ty and Torrance: Wassup, Darnell! Welcome home!

Darnell: Happy to be home. I appreciate y'all. Really.

Ty: Don't even mention it!

Darnell: Where's Takiya?

Mama Lee: She said she's going to be a little late. She's going to school for real estate.

Darnell: When did she start that?

Mama Lee: Last week. I wonder why she didn't tell you.

Darnell: I wonder why too.

Mama Lee: Well let's not worry about that. Go get something to eat. Rich, go ahead and turn that music up! We're about to get this party started!

Michael Jackson- Beat It, Everybody's dancing. Tellic walks outside to get something from the car as a car is pulling up as soon as he reaches his car.

Quincy: Yo, Tellie!

Tellie: Yo, Quincy, wassup.

Tellie says brushing Quincy off.

Quincy: Yoo come here. Let me holla at you.

Tellie hops in the car with Quincy. Quincy parks a few houses down.

Tellie: What's happening, Quincy?

Quincy: Word on the street, your boy is a snitch.

Tellie: *makes a confused face, furrowed eyebrows, slant mouth* Say what?

Quincy: Yeah! How do you think that snitch, Darnell, got out waaaay before Mel and Quel, when they got arrested at the same time with the same exact charges? Don't add up if you ask me.

Tellie: I'm saying though. What did you hear exactly?

Quincy: You know him and QC had that lil beef or whatever back about the years ago about some money. Darnell brought that up to the Fed.

Tellie: What?

Quincy: So right after that, the feds went on the block looking specifically for QC. Apparently when they were in the investigation room, one of the officers slipped up and said Darnell's name.

Tellie: Noo.

Quincy: Say Darnell told them all about QC's lil spots and blocks for a shorter sentence.

Tellie: Nooo.

Quincy: Yeah. It's typed up in black ni. Ain't no denying it. I know they were never cool, but the rule is "do not snitch". So you better watch your back because he might mess around and snitch on his own people if the price is right.

Tellie: SHOOT! I'm not even serving anymore though. I'm about to move to Atlanta to start a record label.

Quincy: Stop lying!

Tellie: I'm not lying. I move next month. I have two artists right now, but that's all I need because they're both fire!

Quincy: Boy that jive is not finna work. It's too many people in Atlanta already doing that.

Tellie: Nah, my artists have their own unique styles, way different from those other rappers. Plus, they're fire with it. So I believe in them, and God got me. So I don't even need your negative energy.

Quincy: Yeah whatever, dreamer. You're behind is going to be on that nine to five soon just like the rest of us with failed dreams. You ain't slanging no more either? *bust out laughing* Ole dreaming self. This Savannah. Nothing don't come up from outta here.

Tellie: Alright. I'll holla at you. *Tellie gets out car* The haters and non-believers can kiss my black backside. I have to go see what Darnell has going on *walks in door, taps Darnell's shoulder* Yo, boy. Let me holla at you real quick. *They walk outside.*

Darnell: Wassup?

Tellie: What gives, Darnell? I heard you snitched on QC.

Darnell: *looking around and skeptical* Boy who told you that!?

Tellie: Stop trying to make yourself look better than what you actually are. You know you don't have to lie to me. I can see right through you.

Darnell: You remember he crossed me out of 250 thousand dollars. I had to get his thieving behind back. I am not about to sit in that jail when I know how to get out. I have kids to take care of.

Tellie: Come on, cousin. We don't get down like that.

Darnell: I'm saying, Tellie. It isn't like I snitched on our own friends.

Tellie: That boy is close enough to your own tribe *taps hand, referring to skin color* You know that painful feeling, to be snatched away from your family, to be locked up like a zoo animal, only to see your kids behind a glass this thick. Come on, man. You don't cause that pain to anybody else. That's what the cops are already doing and tricking you to do the same thing. Yeah, they let you out only to be paying you more attention on these streets, so they can lock your ignorant behind right back up again. I'm outta here, Darnell. I can't even rock like that. Don't call my phone.

Darnell: SHOOT, Tellie. We have been down since we were kids. You're just going to stunt on me like that?

Tellie: It's funny how you were quick to bring up T-note, but how did you forget to mention yourself? Take care, Darnell.

Darnell: Nah! You don't even have to act like that. Tellie! Tellie!

Tellie gets in his car and drives off. Takiya pulls up, hops out and runs to Darnell, smiling.

Takyia: Baby!!

Darnell: Wassup, girl!

Takyia: I missed you so much!

Darnell: You know I missed you too, but why didn't you tell me you were in school?

Takyia: I didn't want to tell you until you got home, to tell you I brought us a new home.

Darnell: What!?

Takyia: Yeah! I was at the grocery store when I ran into this real estate agent. He was telling me all about how real estate works and how much money you can make. So I started classes last week. Once I'm finished, I'll be able to start my own real estate agency. I can buy move-in ready homes, or I can buy and flip homes. It's a lot of money in real estate.

Darnell: Definitely, but you said you brought us a house?

Takyia: Oh, yes! I did. The real estate agent I ran into gave me an amazing discount on a house in The Landings. I couldn't pass up the offer.

Darnell: The Landings! With all those white folks? Takyia, you do realize that I sell drugs?

Takyia: That's what I'm saying, Darnell. I want you to quit! There must be something else in this world that interests you! You have to get off these streets, Darnell! It took you away from your family once. Is that your plan again?

Darnell: Are you going to show me the house?

Takyia: Oh it's beautiful, Darnell! *with both hands on his chest as he has both arms wrapped around her petite, lower back.

Less than an hour later, Darnell and Takyia are in the same position, and the three boys are looking confused, in front of their new home.

Takyia: Welcome home, boys!

Keith: Home? This is our house?

Takyia: Yep, and you all have your own rooms and a game room, and there's a pool in the back.

Darnell Jr.: Yayyy!

No. G.: Two Years Later

2000

Darnell is in the old neighborhood with Mel and Quel next to a big white work van. Eight years old Darnell Jr. and seven years old Darius are passing by on their bikes.

Darnell: Y'all come here!

Darius: Yes, Daddy!

Darnell: Put these bookbags on. We are going to play a game. Y'all are going to race, and do not stop until you make it to the house. Take the bags straight to my room. The winner gets the new freshest kicks in-stores right now! Ready?

2 Boys: Yes!

Darnell: On your mark, get set, go!

The boys are racing all the way home with the bookbags. Darnell Jr. wins. They drop their bikes in the front yard and run straight to the bedroom.

Darius: I wonder what's in these bags.

Darnell Jr.: Let's open them. *They open the bookbags, and their jaws drop.* I knew it!

Darius: He told Mommy he wasn't selling drugs anymore.

Darnell Jr.: Don't act like you ain't know the phony pony is a liar, Darius. Plus he makes a bunch of money. Why would he stop?

Darius: How much money do you think he makes?

Darnell: I don't know, but I wanna make the same kind of money he is making.

Darius: How are you going to do that, Darnell Jr.? Daddy is not about to let you sell drugs.

Darnell: You darn right I'm not.

Darnell Jr.: Oh yes you will!

Darnell: Say what!?

Darnell Jr.: If you don't let me sell drugs like you, I'm going to tell Taky that you are still selling them, and I'm going to tell her that you had us racing with them, making us think it was a game.

Darnell: Boy it be your own family.

Darnell Jr.: Think about it. We look like two innocent little boys. The police won't suspect a thing. Plus, you won't have to worry about holding anymore because we can make all the transactions for you. And we can make it seem legal. We can start a carwash with the money and leave the drugs in the cars.

Darnell: *takes the bookbag from Darnell Jr., and he reaches inside* This is a pound.

Seven thirty that night, the three boys and Darnell are in the car, in the garage. Darnell takes the battery out of his cell phone and hides it in the glove compartment so that he could hide his clients and mistresses from Takyia.

Darnell: And you bet not say a word to Takyia!

Darnell Jr. and Darius: Yes, Sir.

Keith: About what?

Darnell Jr.: We'll tell you later.

They walk in the house.

Darnell: Sure does smell good in here!

Darriah: Daddy! *runs to Darnell with open arms*

Darnell: Hey, Daddy's baby! I missed you!

Darius: Hey, Mommy!

Takyia: Hey, my babies!

Keith and Darnell Jr.: Hey, Taky!

Takyia: How was y'alls day?

3 Boys: Good.

Keith: Good. They're making me the first string quarterback!

Takyia: What!!!? That's really good, Keith!

Darnell puts one year old Darriah down, and she runs up to Keith.

Darriah: Hey, G!

Keith: Darriah, my name is Keith.

Darriah: *shake head no* G.

Keith: Okay, Darriah. You can call me G. *hugs her*

Takyia: Y'all go ahead and get cleaned up. Dinner is almost ready.

The three boys run to the bathroom. Once they make it inside, Keith shuts the door.

Keith: Okay, now tell me.

Darnell Jr.: Daddy is letting us help him sell drugs so we can make a bunch of money like him.

Darius: Yep!

Keith: What!? I wanna sell drugs too!

Darnell Jr.: Come on, lil bruh. You are way too talented to sell drugs. You are getting straight A's in school. You are super raw in football, and your mama would kick your butt if she found out. I don't want you worrying about nothing. Let us make the money. You just continue to be a superstar, and we'll take good care of you.

Keith: Alright man but y'all be careful. I don't want y'all going to jail like Daddy.

A week later

Darnell is standing on the block by himself. An unmarked car is the cut watching him. A junkie walks past the car.

Police: Pssst. You wanna make some money?

Five minutes later

Junkie: *walks up to Darnell* Wassup man. Help me out, my guy. I'm feening like a mug.

Darnell: How much do you have?

Junkie: I have $200.

Darnell: Alright. *throws it on the ground and walks off. The policeman jumps out and arrests Darnell. Darnell is getting put in the handcuffs as we fast forward to the jailhouse, in 2015 as the officer is taking the handcuffs off of G's hands.

His facial expression shows that he isn't in the greatest mood as he walks into his cell.

Sanka: How are you feeling today, Young King?

G: I'm feeling low today, Sanka. It's my Junior's first birthday, and I can't be there.

Sanka: I couldn't even picture the feeling. Boy I just thank God I don't have any kids. But it's going to be okay. You only have four more years. That's all, Young King.

G: You make that four sound so smooth.

Sanka: Smoother than nineteen. Ima either be eighty when I get out or dead in this hell.

G: I'll take the four, dawg. Say man, where is that book you were reading last night?

Sanka: Right here.

Lawrence: Excuse me, Son. *G turns to see a officer standing in the doorway* Come let me talk to you right quick.

G walks toward him.

Lawrence: My name is Officer Lawrence Brooks. How are you doing?

He says as he is passing him an envelope.

G: Good, and Thank you.

Lawrence: As I was reading your name, I could help but notice the sender's name. Who is she to you?

G: That's my mama.

Lawrence: I could have been your daddy.

G: What!?

Lawrence: *shakes head, small chuckle* You mama was my lady until she cheated on me with your daddy.

G: Are you kidding me!? My mama cheated on you with my daddy of all people?

Lawrence: Yep. I was crazy bout your mama. Boy she shattered my heart.

G: SHOOT. man, I'm sorry to hear that.

Lawrence: Nah man, don't be. Life goes on. But what are you doing here?

G: *sucks teeth* My son's mother set me up. She was pregnant with my son when I walked in on her downing a bottle of Ciroc and upping that white. I took it from her and left on foot. She called the police on me. She told them I beat her up and all. *He slowly shakes his head.*

Lawrence: Aw shoot. I'm extremely sorry to hear that. How long do you have?

G & G: LIVE WITH NO EDITS

G: Four more years now.

Lawrence: How old is your boy?

G: He turned one year old today. They're throwing my little man a birthday party right now.

Fade to twenty-three year old Darnell Jr. and twenty-two year old Darius walking in Chuck E. Cheese with bookbags and gift bags.

Darnell Jr.: There they go. Darri!!

Darriah: Hey, Darnell Jr.! *smiling, waving them over*

Darius: Hold up. Who the hell invited them? *looking at Takiya and Darnell*

Darnell Jr.: He's their grandchild. Be cool, Darius.

Darius: Yeah iight.

They get over to the family. Sixteen year old Darri is holding Lil G. Darius grabs him, as Darnell is sitting the gifts on the table.

Darius: Wassup, Nephew!

Darnell: Y'all not speaking?

Darnell Jr.: Wassup.

Darius: *nods head* Come on, big man. Let's go play the games.

Qwamaine and Goose (G's bestfriends) walk up. Qwamaine has been G's best friend since they were five years old. He's around 6'1, with a medium brown skin tone, with hazel, greenish eyes. He has a big beard with a low cut, with waves. He's the most laid back person anybody would ever meet. Goose is the total opposite of Qwamaine. He's 5'7, with beautiful, smooth dark skin. He has a tall, nappy fro, with a light fade on the sides and in the back. He's loud and wild.

Goose: Family! (fam-lay)

Darnell Jr.: Wassup, Goose. Wassup, Qwamaine.

Darri: Hey, Goose and Qwamaine.

Qwamaine: Wassup y'all. How are you doing, Mr. Darnell, Mrs. Takiya?

Darnell: Doing well, Qwamaine. How's your grandma?

Qwamaine: She's doing good.

Mrs. and Mr. Topple (Quinita's parents) walk up.

Mrs. Topple: Where's my grand baby!

Mr. Topple: How's everybody doing?

Everybody: Good.

Quinita: Hey, Daddy. He's with Darius, Mama.

Mrs. Topple: Hey, Darnell. How are you living?

Darnell: I'm alive. How are you?

Mrs. Topple: God woke me up this morning and blessed me to see my only grandbaby turn one. I'm doing just fine. If I can just see him.

Darnell Jr.: *walks up to Darius* Say, Mrs. Topple just got here, and she wanna see Lil G.

Darius: Forget her We're playing. *They laugh* Alright. *They're walking*

Darnell Jr.: Say, be cool. Please?

Darius: Boy I'm like an AK-47. You trigger me, I shoot. And a gun doesn't hurt anybody til a human pulls that trigger.

Darnell Jr.: Bruh, I know we only care for Lil G, Qwa, Goose, and Darri, but we're here to celebrate Lil G. Act accordingly.

Mrs. Topple: There goes my grandbaby. Give 'em here.

Darius: Hello. How are you doing?

Mrs. Topple: I'm good, young man. Give me my grand baby.

Mr. Topple: What are you being so rude, Shirley?

Mrs. Topple: Oh! Shut up your old mouth, James. I just want my grandbaby.

Darius puts Lil G on his feet and walks up to where Qwa, Darri, and Goose are sitting.

Darius: Wassup, Qwamaine.

Qwa: Wassup, boyee.

Darius: My boy Goose in the building.

Goose: *singing* And you know I'm finna act a straight donkey [dun-kay]!

Darnell Jr.: I'm about to get some cups.

Qwa: Yeah. Go get that and meet us at the basketball hoops.

Darnell Jr.: Fasho that.

Qwa, Goose, and Darius are walking toward the basketball hoops. Darnell Jr. walks to the counter. Darriah's best friend walks up.

Khadijah: Darri!

Darri: Hey, girl!

Khadijah: Girl, where is Qwa's fine self going?

Darri: Girl, they're going to play basketball.

Darnell Jr.: *walk up to Darri* Say, Darri. *hands her some money* Will you go get us some wings please? Wassup, Kadijah?

Khadijah: Hey, Darnell Jr.

Darri: How many?

Darnell Jr.: A bunch of them. These for you, me, Dijah, Goose, Qwa, Darius, and my boys Cool Pop and Tyree are on the way.

Darri: Alright. * Darnell Jr. walks toward the basketball hoops*

Khadijah: Ooooo hold up! Cool Pop coming too? Girl, I can't even choose!

Darri: Girl first of all, all of them are too old for you.

Khadijah: *sticks out tongue and lift one finger* Aht! Let me stop you right there. Qwa is twenty-one . He ain't nothing but five years older and Cool Pop is seven years older. When I turn twenty, Qwa will be twenty-five. Don't seem too big of a difference to me.

Darriah: We're not talking about when you're twenty. In the present, you're sixteen. So he is not even finna be checking for you.

Khadijah: Girl, first of all, boys our age act too stupid. I need a man that knows how to take care of his lady. Not just take me to the movies.

Darri: Girl, let's go get these wings because you're about to blow me. There goes Cool Pop. Hey, Cool Pop! Hey, Ree! Cool-Pop is 6'7, brown skin with big lips. He has these big, beautiful, brown eyes with the longest, thickest lashes you've ever seen. He also has neat, jet black dreads that flow down his back. They've been calling him Cool-Pop since he was 2 years old, because that's the only food he would ask for by name. Tyree is 5'9, light skinned with a Boosie fade. He's always looking to catch a female, just to get himself some pleasure. He's not the settle down type of guy.

Cool Pop: Wassup, lil Sis!

Tyree: What's good, Sis. *to Khadijah* How are you doing? What's your name?

Khadijah: I'm Khadijah.

Tyree: Nice to meet you. I'm Tyree. So where is everybody at?

Darri: Come on, Tyree.. You know where they're at.

Cool Pop: *slight laugh* Fasho That. Come on, bruh.

Tyree: Aye hold up. Look, Lil G.

They walk up to the family.

Cool Pop: How y'all doing? Wassup, little man.

Tyree: Good afternoon. Lil G, What's good, lil man?

Cool Pop: You're going to love your toys. We'll see you in a minute. * they walk to the basketball hoops*

Darnell Jr. vs. Qwamaine on basketball. Darius is pouring a cup of Patron. Goose has a cup and a handful of money.

Goose: I got next!

Darius: Wassup, Cool Pop! Wassup, Tyree. Y'all get a cup!

Tyree: Fasho that!

Cool Pop: Boy y'all know I'll take all y'all money on this basketball game.

Darnell Jr.: Boy go get you some tokens and run it! All that talking you're doing!

Cool Pop: *laughing* Wassup, boy!

Ten minutes later Cool Pop and Darius hooping. Cool Pop is up 20 points.

Cool Pop: You might as well go ahead and quit now.

Darius: I can't quit, Too Cool. I still got 30 seconds!

Little boy: Come on man. You need to! Y'all hogged the game for 20 minutes! We want to play!

5 little boys: Yeah!

Darius: Alright, man dang! Here! *give Cool-Pop the money*

Cool Pop: Come on, Darri. Let's go get Lil G a big prize with Darius' money.

Everybody is back with the rest of the party.

Mrs. Topple: You guys are too grown to be over there playing on them kids basketball game * rolls eyes*

Tyree: *whisper* Attitude.

Quinita: What you say!?

Darnell Jr. nudges Tyree in the arm as he gives him a look that everybody knows.

Tyree: I didn't say anything.

Mrs. Topple: Bad enough Keith is in jail. Now we have to deal with the rest of his drug dealing homies.

Darnell: Aye ni! You need to respect these...

Mrs. Topple: Respect my behind! Respect your wife, Darnell!

Quinita: You've been waiting all night to say that!

Takyia: Excuse me?

Mrs. Topple: Go ahead, Darnell. Give your wife an EXCUSE as to why you are cheating on her every other day.

Darri: Hey! Now this is not the time and definitely not the place for this foolishness. We are here for Lil G. Now Quinita, light the candles so we can sing Happy Birthday. Please?

Mrs. Topple: Darriah, who do you think you're talking to? Stay in a child's place.

Darius: How can she? You're sitting in it.

Mrs. Topple: I don't have to tolerate the disrespect. Come on, James!

James: No, ni! You're always trying to start something when it's nothing to start.

Quinita, we will have our own birthday party for Kenny next Saturday. I said let's go, James! *stomps off*

James: I'm so sorry y'all. I'm going to walk her to the car, but I'm coming right back. Darriah, please don't sing happy birthday without me.

Quinita: We're going to wait on you, Daddy.

Darriah: You got it, Mr. James.

Quinita: Just back, Daddy!

Darnell Jr.: It's all love here.

Once James returns everybody sings happy birthday when Peaches walks up.

Peaches: Happy birthday dear stepson. *everybody turns to look at her* Happy birthday to you!

Goose: Awe hell.

Qwamaine: *shake head*

Darius: Here comes the drama queen of the hour. *shake head

Darriah: Peaches, don't come here with that messy jive.

Quinita: Peaches? I planned you did not just call my son stepson!?

Peaches: Girl don't act like you don't know who I am. I will most definitely be your son's stepmom really soon, boo. Happy birthday, Lil G!

Quinita: Kenneth, do you know this woman?

Lil G: Yes. That's my daddy's girlfriend.

Peaches: *smiling* G's Girlfriend.

Quinita: Girlfriend!?

Peaches: Yes, honey! *singing* when you were sniffing up the coke, G was buying me the totes! *holding up bags*

Darnell Jr.: Say, why you gotta come here being messy?

Peaches: I ain't being messy. I just thought the baby mama should know.

Quinita: Girl, please. You come up in my son's birthday party, trying to flex talking about G's girlfriend. Hoe, G is in jail. He isn't doing anything for you. If anything, you are losing money putting it on his books, with your stupid self.

Peaches: Girl, you are the reason he is in that situation. You're lucky you ain't dead yet. Only reason they are here is for Lil G! Everybody knows that you set G up. Why do you think his mama is not here? Cause she can't hardly stand your crackhead attitude!

Quinita charges at Peaches. Qwamaine catches her mid-air.

Qwamaine: Gone head ni. For both of y'all be in jail for disorderly conduct.

Goose: And Lil G isn't going to have you much longer *he says looking at Quinita* Because we are not coming to bond you out.

Peaches leaves quietly with a smile.

Khadijah: I ain't heard of none of this to go down at a child's birthday party.

Later on the day, Darnell Jr. is sitting on the porch on the corner of 49th and Bash Street, with Darius.

Darnell Jr.: Man we can't ever seem to have a birthday party without commotion.

G: *is on speaker* You're not lying! Peaches was dirty for that though. The simple fact off is this, I'm not marrying her because messiness follows you. If you were messy then, you're going to be messy now.

Darnell Jr.: Facts!

Darius: That's how it is sometimes, brother. Some people know how to clean up the act very well. Let's just say, she's not marriage material for you. Someone will know exactly who she is and will love her flaws and all. Truth be told, you are marriage material right now anything, but I can guarantee you that you will be one day.

Darnell Jr.: *bust out laughing* That's all you talk about is marriage. When do you think you'll be marriage material, Darius?

G: I'm not going to lie, I would love to get married someday. It could be great when executed correctly.

Darius: I believe when I meet my wife then I will be ready. I truly believe that once that exact moment that God tells you that this is your person, you are supposed to act accordingly from that point forward. Where a lot of people go wrong is that they want to wait until they are in the right place in their life. That's not how it works. You ever notice how the most valuable people come into your life during a storm?

G: I heard that. And I totally agree with you. Just when I was about to start getting depressed in here, I met a friend named Lawrence. I can him Larry. Here's the coolest guy I've ever met in my life. And guess what!

Darnell Jr. And Darius: What!?

G: You guys almost weren't my big brothers.

Darius: Say what, G!

Darnell Jr: What?

G: This random man literally came walking up to me and started talking about how my mother cheated on him with our daddy, and she got pregnant from that one night stand!

Darius: Oh my God, G!! You were destined to be with us. Almost not brothers nothing! You were assigned specially to us.

Darnell Jr.: Swear to God I already knew this! I mean I did but I didn't.

G: Explain.

Darnell Jr.: So when I was eight, I overheard your mama and my mama talking about how she missed this guy named

Larry. She swore she would do anything to get him back, but he wouldn't talk to her. She was so depressed about it too, but she always wanted to be strong for you.

G: I wish I knew. I would have gladly given her a shoulder to cry on because that's what I'm doing for Larry right now. He is still to the day crazy over her. He regrets that he let so much time past, but I told him that I don't think it was a coincidence that he met me when he did. It's looking up for them two. I think they could possibly make it if they were willing to put the past behind them.

Darnell Jr.: Speaking of someone that needs to put the past behind them, Uncle Tellie is in town again.

Darius: Guess what, G.

G: Hold on, Darius. What do you mean by that Darnell Jr?

Darnell Jr.: I guess you were just a little too young to prep all of the family drama back in the early two thousands.

G: Cut it out. I was only two years younger than you.

Darnell Jr.: Yes, but a six year old mind is more mature and understanding than a four year old mind. I was very detail oriented too. So I had to get all of the facts straight just so I could understand clearly. Do you remember right after my sixth birthday party, daddy came home, we got the new house, and we never saw Uncle Tellie in that ever. Not once?

G: I didn't think about it like that.

Darnell Jr.: Exactly! So they had told us that Uncle Tellie moved to Atlanta, but it was deeper than that. So apparently, that was true of course, but the full story goes like this. Someone from their neighborhood told Uncle Tellie that Daddy had been granted early release only because he snitched on this guy that had just ratted him out of two hundred fifty thousand dollars. Uncle Tellie couldn't believe what he was hearing, but then daddy confirmed that it was all true. He cut daddy off immediately. After that Daddy got back in the streets heavy after that. That's how he got locked back up for twelve years that time.

Darius: Uncle Tellie kept in contact with us from pure love. We didn't have anything to do with it, but he said he has nothing to say to our daddy.

Darnell Jr.: And I think he should let the past be the past.

G: I'm still trying to figure out how to do that myself. I seriously don't know. I wouldn't be surprised if he doesn't know how to either. What was your guess what, Darius?

Darius: Uncle Tellie came down the other day. He wants to sign me to his label!

Guard: Hang up the phone. We are about to lock this unit down.

G: That's awesome, Darius. Give it all you got, because I know your talents are real. But we're about to lock down. I love y'all, man, and make sure y'all send me some pictures.

Darnell Jr.: Oh yeah! I'm bout to send them right now through this app. Love you too, family.

Darius: I love you too, G. *phone hangs up, Darnell Jr.'s phone rings immediately*

Darnell Jr.: Yo.

Rob: Where are you at?

Darnell Jr.: On the nine.

Rob: Fasho. I'm bout to pull up for a dub.

Darnell Jr.: Alright. I'm out here. *hangs up phone* Boy you don't have any time to be chilling. You need to be rapping or writing at all times.

Darius: I wrote this rhyme about Daddy the other day.

Darnell Jr.: * shake head* Shhh, that nigga. Let me hear it.

Darius: Drop a beat. *rapping* *I grew up wondering where you at. I grew up wondering how you doing. Only thing you ever taught me, life gone hurt you. Keep it moving. You was always in them streets. You was quick to serve a feen, but you was never there for me or my brother big G. I ain't talking financially, man I'm talking physically. Where was you when a nigga was walking round here snagga teeth. Where were you, when I first threw that ball to my brother D. Had us round here lonely, feening for daddy. You was locked up in that cell and the feds has the key. Had to get it on our own. In them streets, hot as steam, and a nigga cold hearted so I always kept that heat.*

Darnell Jr.: Ooooo cut it out! Boy. you gone take off with that one.

Darius: You like it?

Darnell Jr.: Man, everybody in the hood gone like that.

Darius: *laugh* Fasho. I ain't gone lie, boy. I know one girl that ask everybody she meet *looks Darnell Jr. in the eyes* "You know your daddy?"

Darnell Jr.: *laugh* What?

Darius: It's kinda weird, but at the same time. It's a real issue that needs to be addressed.

Darnell Jr.: Seriously. Some people blame the mothers like "oh you should have never laid up with him" or all that, but they must not realize, the ONLY way she gets pregnant is if he shoots his seed. Then he wants to blame her on some "oh it felt too good to pull out", but when he gets the "I'm pregnant" call, it's "oh it ain't mine" or "I ain't ready for no child." But It's all your fault!

Darius: Then it's ones like ours, who chose the money over his kids and claim it's all for them, but never realize that it's okay to take time off to spend with his family. Life is not all about money. People are forgetting that love is not just a word.

Darnell Jr.: Nah, people don't love anymore. They all use each other to benefit themselves, but when they can't help anymore, they dispose of them like garbage.

Darius: Word. Man, I want real love. I want a real family. Only love I ever got, is from you, the Gs, and Darriah. My mama never showed me love. My other siblings felt like I betrayed them cause I wanted better for myself. But you know what, Takyia hurt me worse than anybody. How do you love me so hard, but the second I do something you don't like, I'm not good enough to be your child? I made you mad because you don't agree with my poor decisions, so you hate me? Like you must have truly felt like that, always.

Darnell Jr.: Yeah man that hurt me too. A child only knows what they're taught or see. When you grow up in a certain environment, most times you just adapt. Then you have the one who is exposed to different things. So they know a little better and want better.

Darius: Like G. His mama definitely showed him a different lifestyle. I just hurt so bad everyday for my brother, because he literally doesn't deserve that. *car pulls up* Who that?

Darnell Jr.: Oh that's Rob. He wants a dub. *walks to the car*

HATE: The Next Day

Keith and Lawrence are sitting together in the jail yard.

Lawrence: So how'd you grow up?

Keith: I grew up well actually. My mama and grandma kept me in church, sports kept me busy, and I kept my circle extremely small, so it would lessen the chances of me getting crossed.

Lawrence: You can look at it that way or you can see it as a greater chance to receive a deeper pain.

G: What do you mean?

Lawrence: Who does your circle consist of?

G: Two brothers, one sister, and my two best friends: Goose and Qwamaine.

Lawrence: Exactly. It's always the ones closest to you that'll hurt you the worst.

G: I hear what you are saying, but I truly believe all my folks are solid.

Lawrence: I'm not going to press the issue. You're the type that has to experience things for yourself. The hard way. But, ALWAYS, expect the unexpected.

G: Oh I definitely do that. So tell me, what was it like to be in love?

Lawrence: Oh man, it's the best feeling in the world. You wake up smiling, go to sleep smiling, got food falling from your mouth cause you smiling while you're eating. And it's even better when the woman is just irresistibly beautiful. You can't take your eyes off of her. But when she returns the favor and you KNOW she feels the exact same way you do, it makes you feel indestructible. Like you can conquer anything in the world, as long as she's standing right there by your side.

G: I want that. I want that real love. Why do you think men look at love like it's only a woman's thing?

Lawrence: I wonder the same thing. I wonder who declared that men are supposed to be tough and emotionless, because we also have feelings. We care too. It's not a "woman's" thing to care. Some women lose good men because he's "too sensitive". To a certain extent, it's understandable, but then maybe she just wants the man to put his hands on her and talk to her like a peasant.

G: It'll never make sense to me.

Lawrence: Life doesn't make much sense to me.

G: You're not lying, because this world is really wicked. Don't nobody wants to see you doing better than them. White folks don't want to see you going good at all. And you can't trust nobody period. I learned that at a young age.

Lawrence: What happened?

G: Growing up, I spent a lot of time at my Daddy's house with my brothers and stepmom. My Daddy was never there. He was always in the streets. So we grew a real bond with his wife. My Daddy messed around and got locked up for twelve years and my brothers took over where he left off. A few years later, my stepmom found out about my brothers and cursed them out like a dog and she told them she hated them. Worst part was my brother Darius didn't really have a mom so he looked at her as his mama. So it hurt me and Darnell Jr., but it destroyed Darius. My brother ain't been right ever since. That boy don't trust a soul.

Lawrence: Dang. That's messed up. No parent wants their child slanging, but because they make a poor decision make you hate em? Nah that ain't right.

G: Yeah. None of us talked to her after that.

Lawrence: How old were you?

G: I was 13, so they were 14 and 15. Then my daddy just came home two years ago. I ain't gone lie, I really ain't wanna kick it with him, but my brothers did, so I thought I'd give him a chance too, but it seems like he didn't want us around. Like we are wanting to talk to him. You know, like get to know him, cause we really don't know the man. But he is giving short answers or he doesn't say anything. And if we don't call him or go see him first, we don't hear from him at all. And I don't like that so I just quit trying.

Lawrence: That's completely understandable. I have never been the type to kiss nobody's behind. You don't show me the same love and respect I show you, then I'm out.

G: Me too.

Lawrence: So did you ever serve?

G: Nah, my brothers didn't want me to. So I worked a regular 9-5 at Herty. What about you? You haven't always been a police officer.

Lawrence: I actually serve right now. This police gig doesn't really pay too much.

G: Oh I know. One dude told me he was a policeman and delivering pizza at the same time.

Lawrence: Seriously, I need to find something else to get into though because even though the money's fast, it's still illegal and I really want to be a great role model for the young men in the black community. They're in desperate need of a black man that they can look up to and respect, because nowadays, the majority of them are growing up without a father or looking up to the drug dealers cause they're the only ones in the hood visible.

G: Exactly. I never had a role model. First, cause I never wanted to be like anybody but me. Second, because nobody was doing something I had never seen before.

Lawrence: Well what interests you?

G: God put us all here for a purpose. I just really enjoy designing clothes.

Lawrence: I haven't found mine yet at all. I know it's not to be a police officer. I actually hate this job. Everyone knows how crooked the police are, but being on the other side, you witness it first hand. I haven't quit yet because I don't know what I want to do yet.

Keep Your Head Up: Two Years Later

Qwamaine visits G in jail. Qwamaine has an angry mug on his face.

G: *smiling* Yooo wassup boy!

Qwa: Wassup, bruh.

G: What's wrong with you, cuz?

Qwa: Man, I just hate to be the one telling you this, but you have to hear it eventually.

G: What it is, bruh?

Qwa: Man. Goose flaw as hell.

G: Come on man, quit holding out. Spit that jive out.

Qwa: Oh it's some jive alright. That boy Goose got Peaches pregnant.

G: WHAT!?

Qwa: I just found out yesterday. This man has been messing with her ever since you got locked up.

G: WHAT IN THE FAKE BROTHERHOOD IS THAT? How is my boy gone diss me like that dirty! He knew how I felt bout shawty. A woman is going to be a woman, but I thought that was a brother! Man, forget this. WHAT THE HELL!?

Qwa: I'm not even going lie to you homie. I beat him up yesterday. I'm talking about, I broke his nose and his jaw. I damn near kilt son, cause he crossed you so he crossed me. Straight up.

G: Ooowee jive boy. That's super flaw.

Qwa: Yeah. I know how you feel, cause I really feel like he did it to me cause you my brother. So we're one. When you hurt, I hurt. That foolishness crushed me yesterday, G. *Pause, G just stares silently* But on the bright side, your mama is in the waiting room with Lil G. He is so big, and he acts just like you! It's crazy!

G: Yeah. I talk to him all the time. That man is hilarious. He acts thirty instead of three.

Qwa: *laugh* Ain't it. I really just came to tell you that. I'm going to head out so you can talk to your folks though.

G: Fasho Qwa. Be safe out there. I love you.

Qwa: God got me. I love you too. Keep your head up. You'll be out soon.

Ten minutes later G is face to face with Lil G.

Lil G: Daddy, when are the police going to let you out of here?

G: *smile* I'll be out right after your 5th birthday. So how many years is that?

Lil G: Ummm...

G: What is 5 take away 3? *holds up 5 fingers, drop down three, leaving up two*

Lil G: Two. Two years Daddy!? That's a long time?

G: Very long, but you have think positively. It's better than when I started this sentence three years ago, and I'll be home to you in just two short years. How's school going?

Lil G: Good. My teacher said that I'm the gold star of the class because I'm smarter than everybody else. I lead my line and everything Daddy!

G: That's really nice, son, but I don't want you to think you're better than anybody. If you have the knowledge others don't, you have to teach them and help them become just as knowledgeable as you are. Understand?

Lil G: Yes sir. Guess what, Daddy! The football coach said he would let me play with his six and under team next year, when I turn four.

G: *shakes head* Noo, Lil G. You can't do that.

Lil G: Why, Daddy?

G: Because you need to play with kids your age and size your first year. You have to understand the concept first. You have to crawl before you walk Lil G.

Lil G: But Daddy, I'm good. I know how to play very well, Daddy. Uncle DJ and Uncle Darius say I play just like you!

G: No, Lil G. You are not ready to play with the bigger boys. You can practice with them, but I don't want you playing in the games. Do you understand me?

Lil G: *drops head* Yes, sir.

G: Let me talk to my Mama. Hey, Mama. How are you doing?

Keyawanna: I'll be doing way better when you get out of here. You don't belong here, Keith.

G: I know. What are the lawyers talking about?

Keyawanna: Child, the people won't even talk to me without $13,000 up front. The one that'll take sixty-five hundred dollars keep saying they can't prove that the drugs belonged to Quinita. These lawyers get on my nerves!

G: *shakes head* It's alright, Mama. I'll be out soon. Everything happens for a reason.

Keyawanna: You think you deserve this?

G: I might be getting punished for something I did in the past. God is not going to put me in this predicament for no reason.

Keyawanna: Well what do you think it is?

G: I've been thinking it's because of the hatred I hold in my heart toward my dad. Maybe he's trying to put me in his shoes and see what it feels like being treated like a caged animal. How being in jail can affect your communication skills, your train of thought, the way you treat others. Some people come in and they lose the little education they have and become a product of this place. They allow the police to lock away their minds along with their bodies. Some people use this as a get away from the real world and better themselves. They take advantage of the books, of other people's mistakes, of their own mistakes and analyze it to become a better person who makes better decisions when they get to experience life outside of this place again.

Keyawanna: Maybe this was a blessing for you.

G: I believe that. I met two men in here that have taught me more in three years than my daddy taught me in my whole life.

Keyawanna: Who?

G: An older Jamaican man name Sanka and Lawrence *lifts eyebrow*

Keyawanna: What Lawrence?

G: I think you should call him. He actually needs you to call him, and I feel like you need him too. Everybody needs love, Mama. He really adores you, you know. He may not trust you, but you can earn that back, especially if you want it as bad as you need it.

Keyawanna: Keith, that man doesn't want me.

G: Mama, I talk to this man every single day. I know what he wants. If you wanna die alone without his love, so be it. But if not, he goes to the jazz bar on Broughton Street, every Thursday evening at six by himself. That's all ima say. How is Grandma doing?

Keyawanna: She is doing well. She says she wants to see you, just not under these conditions. So she says a prayer every night for God to keep her here until you get out. Keith, I love that man. I'm sure what happened between us was real. I don't understand how he could just leave me like that. No form of communication at all. It hurts me that I hurt him, but I feel as if he could have at least had one conversation with me in twenty-three years.

G: I don't blame her. I wouldn't want to see myself like this either. But mama, I'm trying to tell you. He's ready to talk. Please go see him. Do it for Lil G. He needs a granddaddy. A real stand up guy, and I believe that he is the man for that position in our family. We all deserve each other's love.

Keyawanna: I love how positive you are, Keith. You're really making me feel good cause I wasn't feeling so well today.

G: Guess what, Mama.

Keyawanna: What?

G: Goose has been messing with Peaches since I got locked up. Now she's pregnant.

Keyawanna: WHAT!!!?? No she didn't! No wonder she hadn't been coming around in the past couple months. She used to come to see me all the time. And Goose!? Y'all been friends since little league. Well, I be darn! Distance always reveals your real friends.

G: Sure do. I'm not even going to worried about it though. You and Lil G just made up my day.

Keyawanna: When did you find this out?

G: Qwamaine just left from telling me.

Keyawanna: I pray Qwamaine doesn't ever cross you. I love him.

G: Yeah. That's my boy, but you never know. But I don't think he will.

Keyawanna: Only time will tell.

two minutes left on video visit

Keyawanna: Okay, baby. I will see you next week. I'm going to let Kenneth talk.

G: Alright, Mama. I love you.

Keyawanna: I love you too, baby. Keep being positive. Do you hear me? Here, Kenneth.

G: I didn't mean to upset you, Lil G. It's just Daddy wants to protect you. I want to keep you as safe as possible. But if everybody else thinks you're that good and you feel confident about playing with the big boys, you can.

Lil G: *big smile* Thank you, Daddy! I'm going to show you that I am ready!

G: Yes, son. Do your thing. But make sure you're respecting your elders, and be good in school. Okay?

Lil G: Yes sir.

G & G: LIVE WITH NO EDITS

G: I love you, Little One.

Lil G: I love you too, Daddy. Keep your head up.

G: *smiles* Okay, Lil G.

Dead Wrong: A week later

Goose, his sister, and her baby's father are in the car.

Josh: Say what, Goose? *turns down radio, Kodak Black, Deep in These Streets*

Goose: *jaw wired* I said stop me by the store.

Josh: Oh iight.*turns up radio*

Keisha: Lil Brother, I know you're in pain and all that, but you need to handle this and I mean fast. Because as your sister, you make me look bad if you just let Qwamaine get away with that without any repercussions.

Goose: Oh, I am most def going to straighten that. I'm talking about on sight.

Josh: You better, because if you don't, *sit gun on lap* I will. No need for close range when you got laser power on the fire launcher. *laugh*

Keisha: Goose, look under that seat and get my phone.

Goose: *struggling to get phone*

Keisha: *looking out passenger mirror, as she's parallel parking*

Josh: *looks out passenger window once the car is parked* Well I be damn. *taps Keisha*

Keisha: *devious smile* Well Well Well... Time to pull a joker's cap back, Goose.

Goose: *finally looks up from getting phone* Look at this man. He's on the phone. I'm about to interrupt this whole transaction .

Goose steps out of the car and runs up on Qwamaine.

Goose; I came to correct you about what went down yesterday. I don't tolerate that disrespectful attitude you was giving me yesterday. I didn't no broken jaw bruh! Look at me bruh!

Qwamaine: Look bruh. That was some foul play you pulled on G. That was this man's girl. That was somebody he thought he could trust. Not only that, you were somebody that he was supposed to trust. We are brothers, man! There is a law that enforced brothers to stay away from each other's ladies. You broke the law, so I broke your jaw.

Goose: From my understanding, they were no longer together.

Qwamaine: Where did you get that information from because G seems real surprised that you two were even seeing each other!

Goose: I didn't ask G, but she said they weren't together. So I took my shot. Maybe I should have talked about it with G, but I wanted her bad, so I took her word for it, and she got pregnant.

Qwamaine: Its been three years. How could you keep a secret like that to yourself, but you were so comfortable to tell everybody that she's pregnant. We're still shocked that she's your lady, when she was just with my brother!

In the car

Josh: What is going to? Why are they doing all this talking? It's supposed to be going down. I knew your brother was going to punk out!

Keisha: Would you kill me if I broke your jaw?

Josh: Sure would!

Josh jumps out of the car and shoots Qwamaine dead to the ground. Keisha hops out of the car and grabs Goose by the collard. She yanks him so hard that his body moves in one swift motion straight inside the car. She drives off as fast as she could while Josh grips the back passenger door. He runs and dives in the car headfirst. He struggles with closing the door at first , but then it gets slammed close by a fast vehicle that t-bones the car from one side of the street to the other. It was the police. They saw the whole thing. They saw Goose run up in Qwamaine's face, and they saw Josh jump out of the car to shoot Qwamaine. As one office was about to run toward the crime scene, the other one went to get the car. They were parked in the alley when Keisha was driving past the alley.

They both jumped out of the car with guns pointing to the faces of Josh and Goose.

All three of them are called to get out of the car and onto the ground. They are all arrested immediately for the murder Qwamaine Lawson.

You're A Soldier: The Next Day, Tuesday

Darnell is walking through the metal detector at the jail. He scans his ID, gives it to the guard, and sits down. They call his name and tell him his kiosk number.

G: Daddy.

G says with a smile on his face.

G: I was hoping that you would come see me. I've been needing to talk to you.

Darnell: How are you doing, Son?

G: I'm alive and healthy. I'm grateful. How are you?

Darnell: I'm not doing too good, Son. I came to be the bearer of bad news.

G: What's going on Daddy?

Darnell: Qwamaine's grandma called me last night.

G: Oh, yeah. How is she doing?

Darnell: Physically, she's fine. Emotionally, she is not good at all.

G: What do you mean?

Darnell: G uhh.. They uhh... Qwa got kilt yesterday.

G: What?!

Darnell: They found him by the phone booth in front of Chu's on MLK with his head bust open by a bullet.

G: *scream cry*

Darnell: The police witnessed the whole thing. G, Goose kilt Qwamaine.

G: *cries harder*

Darnell: Him, his sister, and her baby daddy.. *silent as G cries*

What happened, man? Why were they beefing?

G: Qwa found out Goose had been messing with the young lady I was dating before I got locked, and he just got her pregnant. Qwa got upset about that whole situation and broke Goose's nose and jaw.

Darnell: Damn. So you just lost the only two friends you ever had, you still got two years left for a crime you didn't even commit, and on top of that, when you come home you gotta start all over again and not with a clean slate.

Once you get out, these crackers gone make it harder on you, son. They not gone want to give you a job. You can't vote. You gotta report to those probation officers every month.

Son, listen. I know what you're going through. I know what it feels like on that other side and to keep hearing bad news. I've been there. I'm trying to tell you, Son. Trust me, but I want you to know that you are not alone. I'm here for you. Anytime you need to talk, just call me.

But I need you to keep your head up. Things are going to get better. It may take years before they do, but please Son, don't give up. I need you to hang in there. You got my blood flowing through your body, so I know you're a soldier. Please don't fold, son. I love you. Ima come see you next week, and I'm finna put a couple dollars on your book.

G: Thanks, Dad.

Darnell: Alright, Keith.

Get Your Man Back: The Next Day, Wednesday

Keyawanna and her Mama are sitting in Mama J's kitchen.

Keyawanna: Mama J, you remember Keith's friends Qwamaine and Goose?

Mama J: How could I forget? They ate dinner over here like I gave birth to them.

Keyawanna: *shakes head with frown, heavy sigh*

Mama J: What done happen?

Keyawanna: Well apparently Goose has been messing with Peaches ever since Keith got incarcerated.

Mama J: What!? I knew I didn't like neither one of them.

Keyawanna: You did say that.

Mama J: Yes I did, because I didn't like Goose's vibes as they got older, and I told Keith that too. And as for the lil hussie, I didn't like her when I first met her.

Keyawanna: Why, Mama J?

Mama J: She wore too much makeup. Made me feel like she had something to hide. Now I know. She's a two timing, homie hopping tramp!

Keyawanna: He got her pregnant too.

Mama J: Well goodie for her!

Keyawanna: Qwamaine found out and beat Goose so bad that he broke his nose and jaw.

Mama J: That's because Qwamaine is a real friend.

Keyawanna: But it backfired on him because Goose and some other boy kilt Qwamaine the other day.

Mama J: What!!? Not Qwamaine! Lord Jesus! Why Qwamaine, Lord! Lord why! Besides his brothers, Qwamaine was Keith's only real friend. And real friends don't come easily.

Keyawanna: I know that. And once your eyes are open to that, your whole mindset changes.

Mama J: That's right. Real friends show real love. Everybody thinks the person they love is going to play them, so they cross them first; but in reality, the other person never even had intentions on hurting em.

Keyawanna: That's because everybody has been hurt before so everybody has trust issues.

Mama J: If everybody just be loyal and commit to one another, we wouldn't have to worry about none of this. And if you commit and they turn out to be someone you don't see yourself being with, just leave! Ain't no need in cheating. If they aren't satisfying all your needs, leave em alone. You hurt them more by cheating than leaving.

Keyawanna: Keith said Larry asked about me, Mama J.

Mama J: Larry!? Now that's a name I haven't heard in awhile. How's he doing?

Keyawanna: He's doing fine. I ain't gone lie, Mama J, when Keith said his name, it brought back so many feelings.

Mama J: I bet it did. You and that man were head over heels about each other.

Keyawanna: Yeah, well I made a huge mistake.

Mama J: You were young. But since he asked about you, I don't think it's over.

Keyawanna: I cheated on him and had a whole baby with a drug dealing jailbird who was not hardly in my baby's life. How could he forgive me?

Mama J: Seems like you're searching for the wrong person to forgive you.

Keyawanna: What do you mean?

Mama J: You need to forgive yourself, baby. That was twenty-three years ago. Give it to God and let it go. Forgive yourself then go talk to Larry. You need a man. I love you, but I don't wanna see you all the time. I have things to do myself.

Keyawanna: *Laugh* I know it. Keith said he goes to Good Time Jazz Bar on Broughton Street every Thursday evening. I was thinking about going.

Mama J: What is there to think about? Keyawanna gone and talk to God, then go find you something nice to wear to go get your man back.

Keyawanna: *smiles, hugs Mama J* I love you, Mama J.

Mama J: I love you too, Keyawanna.

Hurting On Me:

The Next Day: Thursday, 5:50pm

Keyawanna is sitting in a black Honda Civic, wearing a sexy black dress.

Keyawanna: Oh kg, Lord. I believe this is the right thing to do. I mean, what's the worst that can happen? He could curse me and tell me that he never wants to see me again. *Looks in mirror* Who am I kidding? As good as I look? *smiling* Humble me, Lord. Okay, Keyawanna, get it together. You're going to go in there and apologize. Man, I haven't seen this man in twenty-three years. Man, I'm about to go. I can't handle this. *backs the car up without looking. Hits a man* Oh Jesus! What was that!? *She gets out of her car and run to see* Oh My Gosh!!!

Lawrence: Damn, Keyawanna. You must love to put a hurting on me, Woman.

Keyawanna: Oh my gosh, Larry. I'm so sorry!!!

Lawrence: It was just a bump. I'm okay. How are you doing?

Keyawanna: I'm doing well. You look amazing.

Larry: Oh baby, you're just looking at your reflection. Keyawanna, I've been missing you.

Keyawanna: Larry, I'm so sorry for what I did to you. I know I hurt you, because I still hurt just thinking about it. I just feel so ba...

Larry: Keya, That was twenty-three years ago. Baby, the only thing I'm wondering about is if you're seeing someone right now with your pretty self. Girl, you're so beautiful.

Keyawanna: *Smiling* Thank you. God is giving me the opportunity to see you right now.

Larry: *Smile* Good. Me too. Thank you, Lord. *Hold out bent arm* Would you like to join me for dinner, reckless driver?

She burst into laughter and then jumps into the man she loves arms as she wraps her body around his. He hugs her back so tight.

Keyawanna: Larry, I've missed you so much!

Larry: I missed you too, Keya!

Later on, Keya and Larry are seated at the table together listening to the trumpet player on the stage.

Keyawanna: How did you know Keith was my son?

Larry: I was a temporary replacement for the person responsible for delivering personal mail to the inmates. I "just so happened" to stumble across your handwriting . Til this day your beautiful penmanship still stands out to me, but when I saw your name and almost broke down in tears. I haven't seen or heard your name in 21 years, then all of a sudden, you popped back up. I felt like it was a sign. So I delivered the letter to G personally. I didn't know who I was coming in contact with, but when I saw his face, I knew he was your son. He literally looks just like you.

Keya: Wow. This was definitely my God.

Larry: *smile* Nothing but. So when I got to him, I just looked at him for a little second. Because I saw you all in his face. When I saw him, I felt a shift in the atmosphere. It felt like a powerful force pushed me toward him. Keya, the next thing out of my mouth was "I could have been your daddy."

He busted out laughing as she let out a loud screeching laugh. She apologizes as she continues to laugh at her former lover.* Larry! What did he say? Because Keith has a very smart mouth.

Larry: Nothing out of the way, Keya He was just like, "what!!" I shocked him. He could barely say that word. Then I told him our story. I felt like it was truly meant to be because we connected so well immediately.

Keya: I already told you my Great God set this up.

Larry: I believe you too because we've gotten so close. I feel like the boy is mine, but that's just how God works. He took my rib and made you. So rather that's my seed or not, he's still apart of me because he came from you.

Keyawanna: I'm so stupid for letting you stay away from me for twenty-three years. But you know what. I'm older and wiser. I'm not making the same mistake twice.

Larry: Keya, I know this might be a stretch, but I don't want to lose you again. I nearly lost my mind the first time, but I turned to God. He healed me. I forgave you and now I want you back, but just for me. I will not share you. I will not have only half of you. I need you, Keya, and if you give me a chance, I'll show you that you need me too. *Get on one knee* Will you be my wife, Keyawanna?

Keyawanna: *crying* Oh my gosh, Larry. This was so fast. Let me think about it... *Laugh* Yes! Yes Larry! Yes!

Larry: *smiling hard* I'll buy you a ring in the morning. I love you so much. I love you so much Keyawanna!

Keyawanna: I love you more!

The next morning, Mama J and Larry are standing next to each other in the jewelry store, looking at the engagement rings.

Larry: What do you think about this one, Mama J.?

Mama J: That one's nice, but I like this one.

Larry: Oooo Mama J., look at this one!

Mama J: Oh yeah, Larry. That one is really nice. I like that one.

Keyawanna: *clears throat* Ummm, y'all acting like I'm not even here. I'm the one wearing it for the rest of my life.

Larry: Awww, you're right baby. Which one do you like?

Keyawanna: *scanning rings, then stop and eyes get big* I want this one! This is the one! May I see this one please?

Mama J: Oh now that is beautiful! Just gorgeous!

Ring associate: What size do you need?

Keyawanna: Size six and a half!

Larry: Well, what else is there to say, other than *he gets on one knee* Will you marry me?

Keyawanna: Yes! Yes! Three times yes!

Larry: Thank you Jesus for sending her back to me! *He grabs on her waist as he kisses the top of her head.

The Hole: The Next Day, Saturday

G: Wassup, Lawrence? *looks pale*

Larry: *glowing* Say man. What's the matter with you?

G: I just found out my best friend, Goose, got my old girl, Peaches, pregnant, so my real best friend, Qwamaine, beat him up. Then Goose got Qwamaine kilt.

Larry: What!?

G: Yeah, man. I couldn't stop crying, then I saw you and eased up. Wassup with you though? You look like a light bulb.

Larry: *smiling hard*

G: Come on, man! It's only been like four days since I last saw you. Ain't no way you met a woman, and she got you smiling like that already.

Larry: Nah, I didn't have to meet her. Just an old friend resparked a new light.

G: *Smiling* How do you "re"spark a "new" light?

Larry: Mannn... Your mama is a very special lady.

G: I knew it! So how did it happen?

Larry: Well I was in the parking lot of The Jazz Bar when suddenly, I was hit with a car by a reckless driver. Your mama.

G: My mama hit you with her car!?

Larry: *Laugh* Yeah. She came up there to see me and got scared. So she was trying to back out to leave and she hit me.

G: Look how God works.

Larry: Exactly. But we ended the night engaged.

G: What?! *smiling*

Larry: Yeahhh, Man. *smiling harder*

G: *Slap Larry's hand* That's what I'm talking about boy! What's the next move? Like what's about to happen?

Larry: Well she wants to wait to have the wedding until you come home. So for the first year we decided we are going to get to know one another all over again, but forever this time. Then the next year, we're going to start planning the wedding, and as soon as you get out, we are going to have the wedding.

G: I respect and appreciate that. I'm happy now! I really can't wait! Lil G is going to be be the ring bearer. My mama's best friend's daughter, Lil Kenya is going to be the flower girl.

You guys are going to have some white and pink orchids. My mama loves orchids!

Larry: Shoot, son. I didn't know we hired a wedding planner.

G: *Laugh* My bad, man. You hyped me up. I can't wait til I get married. The way you're glowing, got me craving love.

Larry: Everyday ain't gone be sunshine and rainbows, but if you truly love her, you'll compromise, deal with it, and never give up on her.

G: That's real. Say though. You think they'll let me go to my boy's funeral on Monday?

Larry: I can see about getting that granted, but there are no guarantees at all. I truly am sorry about your loss.

G: Thanks, Dad. I'm just kidding, but I don't want to miss that. His mama was like my mama. He called my grandma his grandma. That was my ride or die literally. Man if I miss that, I'll probably go crazy.

It's now Sunday, the day before Qwamaine's funeral. The men are in the eating hall. Guards come to G and tell him

that they aren't able to grant his request to attend
Qwamaine's funeral.

Jail mate: Shit fuck it. Niggas get kilt everyday. Hopefully
you'll be able to make it to your brothers' funerals.

G: *punch the boy in the mouth. He falls out of his chair and
on the ground. G stands up and stomps the boy in the face a
few times before the guards detain him and carry him out of
there. They throw him in the hole, where he proceeds to
throw a tantrum (screaming, crying, kicking, punching) for
the next five hours*

Visualize a screen is cut into three three equal parts, and
each man comes on one by one.

Tellie: I would like to make...

Larry: I would like to make...

Darnell: I would like to make...

All 3 men: I would like to make a reservation for two please.
Small white girl receptionist on all three parts of the
rectangles and ask "For what time?"

Keyawanna opens the door wearing a black shower cap and
a big furry house robe.

Larry: Aw come on, Baby. You're going to make us late.

He stands in the doorway with the door wide open. On a different side of town in the same city:

Darnell: We're not going to be late, baby. Just let me take care of you for a couple of minutes.

Takyia closes the bathroom door. She's wearing pink panties and a black bra.

Takyia: No, Darnell.

Darnell: *Grabs Takyia from behind * I promise we won't be late. *Kiss her neck*

She looks at the clock on the nightstand. The time reads that they are going to be late rather they do the do or not. At the exact same time, over in Downtown Savannah. Tellie's wife is screaming his name when she accidently kicks the clock off of the nightstand.

Tellie: Shucks! What was that?

Jamaica: It was the clock.

Tellie: Oh, baby. *moan* We're going to be late.

Jamaica: That was confirmed before this. Please satisfy me before we stop. Thank you!

Over near Delesseps Avenue, around about fifteen minutes away from the restaurant, Keyawanna is scrambling to gather all of her belongings as Larry is yelling "Let's goooo Key-a-wan-na" from the bottom of the stairs.

Over in West Savannah, Darnell trips on his pant leg and rolls down the stairs.

Tellie pulls Jamaica from in front of the elevator.
Tellie: We're taking the stairs.
Keyawanna and Larry are sitting in the car. Larry is driving.
Larry: I told you to be ready at seven because our reservation was at 7:30 pm. All I am asking is that you respect the time. I really believe being punctual is a good habit to get into. It's worth it. Can we agree on that, baby? Please.
Keyawanna: Yes, baby. We can agree on that. Thank you.
Larry: You're Welcome.
In a separate household:
Takyia: Darnell, I

Darnell: *buss out laughing* You're so nasty. It's going to be busy tonight.

Jamaica: Oh great. Now we're going to miss our reservation.

Tellie: Who was that saying, "Who cares? Let me catch me before you stop?"

Jamaica: Nooo. I told you before we started we were going to be late. But you insisted that all you needed was a couple minutes.

Takyia: When have you ever only needed a couple of minutes?

Darnell: Aw baby please stop crying. We're almost there.

Tellie: Come on, baby. We're here.

They get out and run to the entrance as Larry and Keya are pulling into the parking lot.

Larry: I bet she made them late too.

Keyawanna: Oh mind your own business, Larry. We're here now.

Tellie: You don't have anything available?

Host: Only our big table, and we keep that open for parties of six or more. You can be seated in the waiting area. Someone will be leaving soon.

As they are walking down to the waiting area, Larry and Keyawanna are walking in the door.

Larry: Good evening. I made a reservation for Brooks.

Host: I'm sorry, Mr. Brooks. You're more than ten minutes late, so we gave away your table. But if you wait in the waiting area, someone should be leaving shortly.

They walk into the waiting area.

Keyawanna: Tellie?

Tellie: Heyyy, Keyawanna! How have you been, girl? *hug her*

Keyawanna: I've been great. This is my fiancé, Lawrence Brooks.

Tellie: Hey, nice to meet you, brother. This is my wife, Jamaica.

Jamaica, Larry, and Keyawanna: Nice to meet you.

Takyia: Darn it, Darnell! I told you we'll be late.

Tellie: Damn. Is this the only restaurant in Savannah?

Keyawanna: Aw hell nah.

Takyia: Is that Tellie?

Tellie: Hey, Takyia. How are you doing?

Takyia: Good. Hey, Keyawanna. How are you?

Keyawanna: Good. Thank you.

Takyia: What a small world.

Larry: Very small.

Jamaica: Well since everybody knows everybody, I'm going to get us that big table. I'm starving. *run to host stand* Hello. We have a party of six.

Host: Okay. You can follow me.

Everybody is walking slow.

Jamaica: Y'all better come on!

Keyawanna whispers to Larry. Darnell whispers to Takyia. Tellie catches up with Jamaica. Then he whispers in her ear.

Tellie: Baby! That's Darnell. My "best friend".

Jamaica: Oh baby, no way! I'm sorry. I didn't know.

Tellie: It's okay, baby. Everything happens just as it's supposed to. Guess what else.

Jamaica: What?

Tellie: Keyawanna is Darnell's baby mama and she was with Lawrence when she got pregnant with Darnell's son.

Jamaica: *drop jaw* No way!! Which one is her son?

Tellie: *Laugh* Shhh. G.

Host: Here you are. Enjoy.

G & G: LIVE WITH NO EDITS

Jamaica: Thank you.

Everybody takes their seats.

Takyia: Well...Good evening, everyone. *everybody speak* I know everyone here isn't on the best terms, but I truly believe God brought us here together, and he doesn't make any mistakes.

Tellie: I believe that too. So I'll start by saying: Darnell, I missed you. But after I heard what I heard, I just couldn't rock like that.

Darnell: And I completely understand that man. I know how you feel, and I'm sorry. I've been reflecting over my life, and I know now that it's time for a change. I want better. I need better because I've realized that a trillion dollars couldn't fill the hold in my heart. I need love from family, friends, and God. I've realized that it's only because of God that I'm still here because I should have died a long time ago.

Tellie: *gets up to hug Darnell. Darnell is crying* I love you, man.

Darnell: I love you too, Tellie man. *sit down* Larry, hear me out. I'm not proud about what happened, but I'm glad of the outcome. I was blessed with an amazing son. I just wish I

170

realized it sooner. Keith giving me the cold shoulder, woke me up for real. He always acted like that with me, but it made me feel bad the other day when I went to see him. Being that his best friend just got kilt, at just twenty-three years old. It made me realize, sometimes, you don't have "your whole life ahead of you". You never know what is going to happen and when.

Everybody: That's right.

Darnell: So Larry. I'm very happy to see you forgave and took her back because everyone needs real love and can't nobody love her better than you. Good luck on your relationship. Uh ohhh, hold up! Is that an engagement ring, Keyawanna?

Keyawanna: *smile hard* Yes, Darnell.

Darnell: Well alright. That's what I'm talking about! This calls for a celebration!

Tellie: Definitely! Excuse me? May we please have seven bottles of your best champagne please? One for each of them and two for me. I'm thirsty. All that running.

Jamaica: *laugh* Oh Tellie, please. Tell them baby.

Tellie: Oh yeah. I just signed Darius three days ago and the first song he dropped apparently has the streets going crazy!!

Takyia: Say what!?

Tellie: Yeah, it's about Darnell not being the father they wanted him to be and apparently everybody has daddy issues. So it's a banger.

Darnell: Damn. I gotta call my son.

Tellie: Not tonight. He's in Atlanta, going club hopping.

Keyawanna: How about we go put on comfortable clothes, grab a big low country boil, turn UGK all the way up and just enjoy life. I'm not in the mood to "behave" in front of all these white folks.

Cut to the three couples in Takyia's backyard with a big white table filled with seafood. UGK International Player Anthem is blasting through the speakers. Tellie is wearing dark blue jeans and a Real Riders Record Label t-shirt. Darnell is in yellow gym shorts and a black tank top. Larry has on gray sweatpants and a white crew neck with some black Nike slides with the white check. All the women are wearing tights and a t-shirt. The men and women are on two different sides of the yard..

Jamaica: Now this is amazing! You have two dining areas of your backyard, and yet they feel like two totally different places. This is nice.

Takyia: Thanks, Girl. So how long have you and Tellie been married?

Jamaica: Seven years. He was separated when we met. Do you mind if I talk your head off about it?

Takyia: I don't mind.

Jamaica: So, he has been separated for a little while when I walked inside of his studio looking to offer my services as a food deliverer. I sold them a few meals, gave everybody in the studio my business card, and left. The next day plus everyday after that Tellie called me asking for food.

That went on for about a month before he asked me to deliver it to his house. He asked me to come inside to wait for payment. He gave me the money, but the conversation just began. I ended up staying there for at least two hours. After that day, we were inseparable. He called me. I started calling him. We would hang out in his house after work for hours.

It was pure joy. We watched tv, talked for hours, played instruments, painted pictures, read the Bible, baked cakes, and ate good for a good year. After that, we considered each other best friends. And we never once talked about his marriage. I only considered him a friend because of it.

But life changed after a few months. I helped him move into a bigger place. I catered his birthday party at this new house, and that's the day that I fell in love with him. We actually started going out on dates, holding, hugging, and day by day building up the courage to make love.

That went on for another year. It was phenomenal, until it wasn't. He tried divorcing her three times in one year, and she absolutely refused to sign the divorce each and every time. He became so frustrated with the entire situation, that it was hindering the good relationship between us.

He started distancing himself. He grew quiet. He didn't have much to say to anybody. He would sit in silence for hours. He probably cried, but I wouldn't know because I was barely seeing him anymore. He barely called. He barely came over to my place, and I never went over to his. He worked, worked, and worked so much more.

I was missing him like crazy, but this situation was eating him alive. He wasn't himself, and I grew impatient with the entire situation. Eventually, God worked it out for the good. He was divorced. We got married not long after that, and now it's seven years later, and we're happier than we've ever been.

Keyawanna: Girl I know that feeling. Ever since I've been back with Larry, I have a glow that wasn't there before.

Takyia: Can I be honest? I was falling out of love with Darnell when he came home from doing those twelve years. He was institutionalized. It was killing me. I had already been alone for twelve years. Then he came home acting crazy.

Jamaica: Did you ever step outside of your marriage?

Takyia: That's really none of your business, but for the record, no I did not.

Jamaica: You're right. I'm sorry. I completely overstepped my boundaries. After all, I just met you today.

Takyia: It's okay. When he was gone, I was so depressed. It doesn't make it any better that I lost the boys. I was just going through so much. And I tried my best to hide it from Darriah. I definitely had to keep pushing to provide for her, so I really didn't have any time to mope around.

Keyawanna: I was depressed just recently. My only child is serving five years for a crime he didn't commit. And I couldn't even afford a decent lawyer. My mama was sick, and I was this close to losing her. I was also craving for a man to hold me and love me. And on top of all of that, I was going to a job that I hated, just to pay for a house that I can barely relax in. I just really didn't wanna live anymore.

Jamaica: Girl, tell me about it. I actually tried to commit suicide. I swallowed every pill in the house. It was like three hundred pills and I washed them down with Pine Sol, but I'm standing here today, so it obviously didn't work. But once I realized I wasn't dead, I knew that I wanted to live life like I wanted to. Not how someone else wanted me to live. As women, we live for everyone except ourselves. We have to take care of the kids, the parents, the husband or boyfriend.

Do all the cooking and cleaning, go to two or three jobs.
Sometimes we just need a BREAK!!

Takyia: Ugh!! You can say that again. A break from reality.
Let's go out of town! We can take the men or we can make it
just a ladies' vacation.

Keyawanna: I like that idea. Just a ladies' vacation. I'm
definitely down for it.

Jamaica: Me too!

With The Police:

The next Saturday, 12pm

Darriah is on the phone with Khadijah.

Darriah: We're almost on the way.

Khadijah: Where are you now?

Darriah: I'm about to walk in Quinita's front door right now. This woman never locks her door.

Darriah silently walks in the door, Quinita has her back to the door while she has her friend Tanya on speaker phone.

Quinita: Tanya, G coming home soon. I hope he has somewhere to stay because it won't be with me.

Tanya: Lil G's daddy is about to come home?

Quinita: Girl yes, and as you can tell by the tone of my voice, I am not happy about it.

Darriah is so stunned by Quinita's words that she pulls out her phone to see what else she would catch her saying.

Quinita: That's why I got his ass sent to jail in the first place.

Tanya: Why not? This man is about to be freed from prison, and help you raise your son! Why wouldn't you be happy about that?

Quinita: That is exactly why I set him up to go to prison! Girl, that man does not give a flock of pigeons about me! All he cares about is this cry addict, arrogant, attitude having little boy. He doesn't care about me so why should I care about him? I purposely put him in a place where everybody will forget about him! He's too controlling and all too serious for me.

Tanya: Ohh uhh uhh. I didn't know all of that ni, Quinita. You can go ahead and lose my number. You were wrong for that.

Tany disconnects the phone call. Darriah turns off the video, runs and attacks Quinita. She beats her down. She chases her to her bedroom, and tells her to shut up before Lil G hears them. He is asleep in his room. She shuts his door. And beats the breaks off of her again.

Darriah: You had this coming. I already knew you set him up because my brother told us and asked us not to retaliate, but you're on the phone bragging to your home girls about how much you hate your son! I couldn't honor G's request any longer. That is my nephew! I love that little boy past death. Now that I know you don't want him, I'm taking him with me. Darriah grabs Lil G's bag and throws all of his clothes and shoes in it. Then she grabs Lil G and leaves.

At the same time, in Atlanta: Darius, Darnell Jr., Tyree, who is asleep, and Cool-Pop are all at Tellie's house in the living room. when they receive and video message from their younger sister, Darriah!

Darius: ARE YOU FREAKING KIDDING ME! This is exactly what we needed!!!!!!!

Darnell Jr.: Man, God took his sweet time creating Darriah. He is a blessing from heaven. That lawyer's crying about they can't prove my man's innocence, being that they caught it on him. I got something for him now.

Cool-Pop: Nah. Forget about them, I met somebody yesterday y'all probably know him! Matter of a fact, Do y'all remember Aaron Walker from Marshpoint?

Darnell Jr.: Yeah, I remember him. That was a cool brother.

Cool-Pop: Okay. Okay. His lil brother David is a lawyer now. David went to school with G!

Darius: Went to school with G!!? That was G's best man! They rocked tight all throughout elementary school. G never said what happened between them, but it broke up their friendship.

Darnell Jr,: G told me that he lied too much.

Darius: Well now we see why, and it works out in our favor.

Cool=Pop: I have his number, we can call him right now!

180

Darius: Call him! We have whatever he charge. That's an investment! G is about to get that money! Everybody knows it too! Don't sleep on G.

Darnell Jr.: G always stood for Genius. Our little brother is an intelligent, natural born hustler. He's going to make his visions come true.

Cool-Pop: Hello. I'd like an appointment with Mr. David Walker. I'd like to discuss my case with him.

Darnell Jr.: This is going to be amazing to have G back home with us. It's about to be so positive in here. I can feel it.

Cool-Pop: Tomorrow morning at nine o'clock works perfectly. Thank you.

Darius: Let's go to the mall to get outfits for court. G's coming home y'all!

Darnell Jr.: Matter of a fact, let's go for a shopping spree for G!

Cool-Pop: And Lil G! He needs to be just as fresh as his daddy.

Darriah is now meeting Khadijah and her two little cousins at Chuck E. Cheese. Darriah is walking in. Khadijah is already there.

Khadijah: Sis!

Darriah: *sit down* Hey, girl.

Khadijah: Girl, so what happened!?

Darriah: I beat that woman like a record, tore her up!

Khadijah: Now, Darriah! You know she has a reputation with the police!

Darriah: She's going to have more than that. She is going to have a record with the police. Look at this evidence.

Khadijah: Are you kidding me! Arrogant!? Controlling!!? Is that any reason to send somebody to jail!?! Are you kidding me!!!?

Darriah: Me, my mama, daddy, and brothers are going to have to work out a schedule until G comes home because I don't want Lil G over there period.

Khadijah: Darriah. I am shocked!

Darriah: Lil G is more mine than anybody's and she knows that. I'm not ever about to worry about nothing. My big brother is coming home.

Kadijah is screaming to the top of her lungs! Then Darriah phone rings.

Darriah: Girl, be quiet. It's Darius. Hello?

Darius: Lil Sis, wassup?

Darriah: Hey Darius. What's going on?

Darius: What are you doing?

Darriah: Me and Dijah brought the kids to Chuck E. Cheese. What are you doing?

Darius: We are at the store. I'm finna send you two plane tickets for you and Khadijah to come up here with us. We are going to meet with the lawyer first thing in the morning. You are G's key witness, so you are going to need to testify.

Darriah: What time?

Darius: The plane takes off in two hours and you'll be here in thirty minutes. So go ahead and drop the kids off. Don't worry about packing any bags for nothing. Y'all just come on.

Darriah: Alright. See you soon. Come on. Darius just got us some plane tickets to go come to Atlanta with them.

Khadijah: Whoop! Time to go! My crew, let's go!

Three hours later, Darius, Darnell Jr., Cool-Pop, and Tyree are picking the girls up from the airport. Everybody is ecstatic to see one another.

Darius: Wassup, Darriah!

Cool-Pop: Lil Sis!

Darnell Jr.: Darri, Dijah, wassup!?

Tyree: Damn, there she goes again. Khadijah, how are you doing?

Darriah and Khadijah: *hug and speak to everybody*

Darius: We're about to go back to the mall to get you ladies some clothes and things. Then we are going to the club tonight. Then I have to go to the studio. This stuff is not cheap.

Darriah: So you're officially moving here?

Darius: Yeah, Darri. All of us are. We are getting out of the drug game and turning this dirty money clean.

Darriah: I wanna move too then.

Darius: Well you know you have to ask your mama first or you can wait until you graduate. We really want you here with us too though.

Darriah: We'll figure about the logistics of everything in the morning. I want to party.

Darnell Jr.: She said what?

Darriah: I feel so good, y'all! Our brother is about to come home! G is about to be a Daddy in real time! We're all responsible adults! And we are living our best lives! I am going somewhere to dance tonight!

Darius: I pray that you enjoy yourself tonight. You deserve it. So where is Lil G at?

Darriah: With my mama..

Cool-Pop: We might as well bring Lil G up here with us to until G comes home. During the day, he's going to be at daycare. When he gets out, with all five of us here, he's definitely going to be looked after.

Tyree: Fasho that. Lil G can't grow up being acting like his mama. I refuse to let that happen.

Darnell Jr.: Oh everything! Boy I can't wait til my brother get home. My lil mans needs his daddy, and my mans need his son.

Darius: We have to talk to Ms. Keya about this too. You know she needs to see Lil G as frequently as possible..

Darnell Jr.: We love traveling. It's nothing to drive Lil G to her.

In Savannah, Tellie and Darnell are in the Oglethorpe mall.

Darnell: Man, I need a new phone. I've been trying to hold on to this iPhone six for the longest.

Tellie: Guess what. It's nothing wrong with that. Apple programs those phones to only last for a certain amount of time, so you are required to spend more money on their "latest and greatest" piece of technology.

Darnell: And that's not a problem because they have to stay in business, but I'm not going to be one of the ridiculous people who falls for one of those gimmicks.

Tellie: Although I am financially free as I want to be, I am not about to constantly spend a thousand dollars on no damn cell phone either. I mean, it's just ridiculous. On top of paying for the phone, you have to pay for the service too. And they are waxing at Verizon.

Darnell: On everything!! I really just don't understand phone companies. You can pay your bill on time every month, but the second you miss one payment, they cut your phone slap off. Like they're making billions of dollars on a daily basis because everybody has a different payment date. So you're telling me, my one hundred dollars is going to keep you from going bankrupt?

Tellie: You really can't even breathe right if you ain't got no money! I was talking to my lil cousin the other day, right. He says he bought an Xbox.

Darnell: Oh them things expensive!

Tellie: Tell me about it! I didn't even know that either. Because you know I have never really been on video games like that. This man said the console itself is five hundred dollars. Then the games are around sixty.

Darnell: And you need more than one game.

Tellie: Then on top of that, you have to pay for extra controllers, accessories, and all kinds of other stuff. On top of that; you have to pay for the internet service, but on top of that, you have to pay for a subscription!

Darnell: A subscription for what!?

Tellie: To play online with other people and access the internet.

Darnell: Damn man. Suppliers know how to make consumers spend a dollar!

Tellie: You ain't lying! Ooowe jive! Look at Mel and Quel. I haven't seen them boys since back then.

Darnell: Yeah, me either really. After they got out, they were still in and out of jail so I had to cut all toxic off. I was trying to get my life together, and I couldn't surround myself with the same people I was getting in trouble with.

Tellie: Oh yeah. I know about it. Ima go holla at them boys though.

Tellie and Darnell walk up to Mel and Quel.

Tellie: Long time no see.

Quel: Tellie boy, wassup!

Tellie: How y'all boys living?

Mel: Just tryna make a dollar outta fifteen cent. I see y'all boys living the life.

Darnell: I'm just maintaining. Ain't too much going on.

Tellie: It's good to see y'all boys! Let me treat y'all to some lunch.

About an hour later, Tellie, Mel, Quel, and Darnell are at B&D burgers on Abercorn Street.

Tellie: Did y'all ever get married or anything?

Mel: Absolutely not! I am never getting married! I can't trust these women, Tellie! Hard no!

Tellie: Well, what have you been through, Mel?

Mel: Right after I got out of jail from serving 5 years, I ran into one of my old lil flames. I told her that I had just gotten out of jail and pretty much needed a place to lay my head until I got back on my feet. Everything was all good until we became intimate. She got possessive! Out of the blue!!! Where are you at? Who are you with? Let me see your phone! At first, I brushed it off because she was feeding me, gave me a place to stay, let me hold her car, and everything. But I couldn't deal with her controlling me. I was just being controlled by those peace snatching cops. I just wanted to be free.

Tellie: Women could be some manipulative creatures. They like to use men when they're down so they can control them. If you give a woman the chance to tell her friends she's taking care of you, you basically lost your manhood in her eyes. She now is going to look at you as a child and the respect you want, out the window. Forget about it.

Quel: Ain't that the truth.

Mel: So I was laying on the couch one day. I was feeling down all in my bones.

Darnell: Why?

Mel: I realized I wasn't a man. I realized I was just a little boy sucking from a lady's breast just to get full. I had just got out of jail. I was broke. I had nobody to call on. Nobody would hire me. I was feeling real blue, D man.

Darnell: I feel you.

Mel: So I'm sitting on the couch, and she comes in with her homegirls. Out of the blue she started flexing on me. Showing off for her company. Talking about, "Oh look at this bum. Just a sorry excuse for a man.. Sitting on my couch feeling all sorry for himself. He doesn't work. He doesn't cook. He doesn't do anything."

Tellie: How long was this after you moved in?

Mel: A month.

Darnell: A month!!! Bitch how you expect me to get on my feet in one month when I don't have nothing!? It takes time to get back adjusted to the outside world anyway, after being locked up like a zoo animal. A lot changes in five years.

Mel: Exactly! So at first I didn't react. But she continued. She's talking about "He thinks he can just lay around all day and think the lights are going to stay on. Georgia power wants their money every month, or they will disconnect your services. Just like them, I'm going to disconnect from him.

Darnell: Nooo. But she knew what was up in the beginning! She knew what she signed up for when she let you come.

Mel: Bruh, listen to me. I told this woman from the beginning I had just got out of jail, and I don't have anything! She freaking knew! So I was just going to leave, you know what I'm saying. I tried to walk to the door. She runs past me and stands in front of the door talking about where do you think you're going? I told her, I'm just getting out of her presence because obviously I'm not welcomed. She wouldn't let me leave, y'all. Talk about "low down bastard, you gone hear what I got to say" Like just being extra as a sauce for her homegirls.

Quel: Man I hate that type of immaturity! That phony foolishness be pissing me off.

Mel: On everything! So, I tried hard not to let the demon get a reaction out of me, but then she said, "I heard you killed your mama. She realized she raised a useless, dirty, broke, good for nothing, ugly, black bastard, and it broke her heart and she died!"

Darnell: Oh that's cold!

Quel: This man's mama died from cancer while he was in jail..

Tellie: *Loud gasp*

Mel: I swear to God, I tried everything in my power not to body slam that woman! I was tired of jail. I didn't want to go back, and if I hit her, that's where I would be. Boy, I slung her by her arms from in front of the door and left. I came back the next day to get my clothes and shoes. She had my clothes and shoes in a big black trash bag burned to pieces. I swear to God that hurt me to the core. So a few weeks later, I went and burned her house down.

Darnell: What!

Tellie: Noooo, Mel!

Quel: Damn, lil bruh. I probably would have done the same thing.

Tellie: I'm saying, Mel, you don't think you were wrong for setting the girl's house on fire?

Mel: Say look, Tellie. That was some real foul mess she pulled on me. Real foul. You ain't never had a woman burn up everything you owned. You don't know the pain she brought on me man.

Darnell: *Laugh* Boy you is still the same wild dude. You ain't gone never change.

Mel: I don't know how to change, Darnell. Being locked up corrupted my mind, my spirit, and my pockets. While I was in there, we were slaves. We did work that they pay $30 an hour for, for free. I came home and tried to get a job, and they denied me because of my record.

Quel: Man I already know what is going on behind that barbed wire fence. It corrupts you because that's what it was designed to do. They hide you away for 23 hours a day. They feed you food that they wouldn't even feed their dogs. They treat you as if you're the absolute worst thing in the world. You're not a person. You're not a human. You're a thing.

Darnell: Sho right. *Shake head*

Tellie: That might be one of the worst experiences anybody has to endure. I want to start a program for young boys and teenage boys. They aren't receiving the proper education. Not in school and definitely not at home.

Darnell: Most of them don't have decent role models to look up to. They listen to the music and now the whole world is on drugs, killing their own family, robbing people that's just as broke as they are. I mean it's crazy out here.

Quel: That's what I'm saying. We gotta do something about it. What type of program are you talking about, Tellie?

Tellie: I want to start a program where we recruit misguided young boys, give them the education we wish somebody would have given us as kids. We'll take them out on lil field trips. This is a program that will try its hardest to keep them out of prison. I also want to teach them about how to treat a woman, because the music degrades women and now women are degrading themselves.

Mel: I swear! I remember when you tried everything to see a woman in some lingerie. Now these girls are wearing them outside as outfits.

Quel: Don't even get me started on the Instagram women. Everybody thinks they are a model. They round here showing their behinds to the whole world.

Darnell: That's why I made a fake Instagram to watch Ri. She doesn't know I'm watching. That's how you catch them in the act. Because if she knows, she'll filter everything.

Tellie: Sure will, but Riri is a good girl. I do not think that you have to worry about her at all.

Darnell: Nah I don't. She's trustworthy, dependable, responsible, and respectful. You know what. I was there for her. I made sure she knew how a man should treat her. I made sure she knew how a lady conducts herself in public. And I always give her the explicit version, because life doesn't have a censored version.

Quel: Live with no edits. I never wanted to have kids because to be honest, I don't want my sons to be like me and I don't want my daughters to date anybody like me. That's why I'm a virgin til this day.

Tellie: That's real, Quel. That's the first time I've ever heard that put like that.

Mel: I never wanted kids because I never met a woman I want my daughter to be like. I've been waiting for the perfect woman to mother my children, but then I realized that I can't expect a good woman when I'm not a good man. I'm not financially stable enough to carry my family on my back.

Darnell: I have a family, but I don't even treat them right. My sons can't stand my oxygen, and my wife seems unhappy quite often. I just really have to sit down with myself and analyze everything that I don't like about myself and everything they don't like about me, and change.

Tellie: Change is always good. There is always room for improvement. There's always ways to make things better.

Darnell: Exactly. So I'm going to make a change. For God, my wife, my daughter, my sons, and for myself. I want more out of life. Love. Love is what I need.

Mel: Real love. I have trust issues, but I ain't gone lie, I want to experience real love so bad. I know it's a woman just perfect for me. And I want to find her.

Quel: I sure do want to find mine. I think if I have the right woman, she can help guide me in the right direction. I want to be a better man too.

196

Tellie: Get a relationship with God, and He will make you the better men that you want to be. But it takes time, patience and will power. And you have to trust that He will do it. I know for a fact He will, so trust. Once you become that man, we'll start the program.

Everybody: I'm down.

Tellie: Fasho that.

Nine Years Older: One Month Later

Darius, Darnell Jr, Cool-Pop, Tyree, Darriah, and Khadijah are at one of Tellie's properties in the kitchen. Darriah is cooking salmon cakes and grits. It smells marvelous in there from the sautéed onions and bell peppers. Darius is packing a backpack with a laptop and chargers.

Darius: I'm about to get ready to go to the studio y'all boys. Darnell Jr., are you coming with me?

Darnell Jr.: Yeah, I'm coming.

Darius: Ri, Uncle Tellie left all the keys to his cars in the room around the corner, if you ladies want to go anywhere. *He hands her some money* Have fun! Come on, Junior.

Darriah: Come on. Dijah! Let's see what our options are. *run to other room*

Tyree: Say, Cool-Pop.

Cool-Pop: Wassup, Re?

Tyree: I'm not one even lie to you. I'm feeling Khadijah.

Cool-Pop: I don't blame you. She's pretty. She is young, yet very mature, and fun to be around. She's not an airhead like most girls. Darriah trusts her so you know she is cool. Go for it.

Tyree: For real because Ri doesn't trust anybody. But the way you just described her seemed to me like you've been thinking about her already. Have you?

Cool-Pop: Not in the manner that you have been thinking about her. Me myself, I am not attracted to her in that sense. I know I'm not ready to settle down. So I'm not pursuing relationships. Sure seems like a sweet girl for you though.

Tyree: I can dig that, but here's my dilemma. I feel bad about my feelings towards her because she is only sixteen. I'm nine years older than her.

Cool-pop: Well, let me ask you this. For that split second, how did you feel when you thought I wanted her.

Tyree: I quickly got upset for that split second. I feel like she's supposed to be for me.

Cool-pop: Pursue the relationship. Just see how it turn out for you.

I Love You Lawrence Brooks: One Year Later

Larry and Keya are at Ms. Polly's Bakery.

Keyawanna: May I have one vanilla and one strawberry cupcake.

Larry: And I would like a slice of key lime cake and a slice of lemon cake. That lemon be bussing!

They get their desserts and they wait to eat them. Once they get home, they walk outside Larry's back door that leads to the patio.

Larry: Baby, this year literally flew by!

Keyawanna: That's the truth! It's time to start planning the wedding. Keith is getting ready to come home. I mean everything is just going great! I pray to God it stays this great.

Larry: My life will always be great as long as you're in it.

Keyawanna: *Blush* You don't think you'll get tired of me?

Larry: Do you ever get tired of breathing? Do you ever get tired of waking up? Huh!? Do you ever get tired of praising God? Do you? Do you ever get tired of being alive Keyawanna?

Keyawanna: No.

Larry: Then I can never get tired of you! Because I am thankful that you share the air that I breathe. You are the first person I want to see when I open my eyes. You are one of the main reasons why I praise God. And as long as you're alive, so am I.

Keyawanna raises her arms to the sky, screaming Thank you, Lord!!! Thank you! Hallelujah thank you! She smiles and looks Lawrence in his eyes.

Keyawanna: You were sent from God himself. I love you, Lawrence Brooks. I love you!

Larry: I love you more, Keya Baby!

He kisses her forehead.

Larry: So when are you going to make an appointment to go dress shopping?

Keyawanna: I have an appointment for next week, Wednesday, at ten am.

Larry: Well somebody's on it!

Keyawanna: Preparation is the key to success. Some situations are designed to go wrong, but it helps to be properly prepared.

Larry: I heard that. Just so you know, the reception venue is booked and paid for. The food will be catered by my younger cousin Chef Londonaire. She has the best food you've ever tasted. And I booked our hotel room and ordered plane tickets for the honeymoon.

Keyawanna: Where are we going?

Larry: We're going to St. Lucia. It's an island right outside of South America. Baby it's beautiful! We're going to leave immediately following the reception.

Keyawanna: Ohhh it's all so real! Everything I've been praying for is now a reality. God definitely works in mysterious ways!

Larry: We were going to meet again regardless, but I wonder how it would have happened if G never got locked up.

Keyawanna: A question that will always remain unanswered. So, baby, how many groomsmen are you trying to have so I can line-up these brides' maids properly?

Larry: G is my best man of course, Corey, Don, and Jess. Four, baby.

Keyawanna: Ooow perfect! Okay so, Tylia is my maid of honor, Shaneka, Toni, and Raquelle. And Tylia's daughter, Kenya, will be the flower girl, and Kenneth is the ring bearer.

Larry: And also Keya, we need to create an entire guest list.

Keya: Okay. Let's get started, but first, can we talk about how delicious this cake is!!?

Larry: Man this cake so good, but it's not even a surprise. Ms. Polly has been the best in the business since the nineteen hundreds.

Keya: Oooo, Larry, it's just so moist and sweet!

25 Years In Prison: On The Same Day

G and Sanka are sitting in their cell.

Sanka: I swear this is getting out of hand! These young guys must have lost their minds. Now they're just killing people for the stupidity of it.

G: I heard they shot him in the face! There's no coming back! Once you're dead, you're dead! Lil bruh was on his way to living out his dream of being a rapper, Sanka. People were enjoying his music. I just can't believe he's gone that fast, at seventeen. Rest in peace to my good friend, Huncho Reese. For real. And Jamar Davis Jr. This life is crazy man.

Sanka: These young dudes are out here wildin like they can't get caught by the feds and get twenty-five years in prison or get caught lacking and do life in the graveyard. These young men need guidance. They are jealous, so they kill. They get embarrassed, so they kill. They get their feelings hurt, so they kill. They need somebody to teach them how to be a man and control their emotions. This foolishness is really upsetting me now. Something has got to be done!

G: I'm not gonna lie. My daddy, uncle, and their childhood friends made a pact to get their lives together and once they become the men that they want to be, they would start a program for young men 5-20 years old. The purpose is to give them the role models that they so desperately need. To educate them on how to be a man that will be a great asset to society. To educate them on how to treat women.

Sanka: That's a good idea! I would like to participate for a while. I just feel so bad today, man.

G: Why? What's wrong?

Sanka: Some days, I'm in good spirits. Some days I just sit here and think like, man, I'm really in this place for another sixteen years. Like God. I seriously could die here. Then it's so awful, they are trying to make us kill ourselves here. But they are not going to get me. I've lived life with financial freedom and literacy. I know it's more to life than this, and I also know that there's a chance that I can actually live through this trying time. And When I get out, I'm going to live life to the fullest. I'm a real survivor. I've been through so much in my life, seen so much cruelty. Another man would have folded. I'm still standing ten toes down, solid.

G: Sanka, you are. For real! The things that you told me you
went through really makes me think, I wonder if I would
have made it through, if I was in your shoes.

Sanka: Young king, you have more heart than men my age.
You handled those four years like a real soldier. You are
going be okay. You stand on loyalty, and you have great
morals and values. You have all the tools you need to be
successful in this world.

G: Thank you. After meeting you and Lawrence, I have
become a better man. I didn't have a father figure in my life.
My brothers and I didn't have anybody that could show us
manly behavior. The only lesson my daddy taught us was to
be independent because you can't depend on anybody. I was
three years old.

Sanka: Well guess what. Now you are fully prepared to be a
free man. I can't wait til you get out of here, G. This is not a
place for a person with your kind of mind. You're very
intelligent and goal driven. You didn't allow them to lock up
your mind with your body. You came in here and learned.
Now you're going to be a better person than when you came
in. That's rare and that's why you don't belong here.

G: I appreciate that, Sanka. We have to get you out of here before sixteen years. You've served forty-four years. You didn't even commit any major crimes to serve sixty years. Come on man. It's 2019! Times have changed. I know we can get you a hearing and try to get you outta here. The judge gotta have some kind of heart.

That night, G calls Darius on the jail phone.

Darius: Yo, yo! Wassup. lil bruh!

G: Wassup, Darius. What do you have going on!?

Darius: Lil bruh I'm in the studio right ni. It's like I'm addicted to this rapping jive. So I be here my whole day, making song after song.

G: That's wassup! You're not supposed to let nobody out work you. The more you work on perfecting your skills, the better you get. Remember that.

Darnell Jr.: G, what's good, lil bruh?

G: Darnell Jr., wassup? I miss y'all boys.

Darnell Jr.: We miss you too, lil bruh. Guess what, though. You're going be out sooner than we thought! We ran into David Walker, remember you old friend that you said lies too

207

much? Well he was just practicing to be a lawyer! I know for a fact that you will be coming home! We have some evidence that will turn your case completely around. Your court date is next week!!!!

G: Boy, quit playing! Ooowe jive! I believe that too!

Darnell Jr.: On everything, brother. I can feel it all in my spirit.

G: Boy, I can't wait! Say though. You think you could get him to bring up my partner's case too? You remember I told you about Sanka?

Darnell Jr.: Sure do. Guess what. Ima call the lawyer soon as we hang up to hop on that too. That man is too old to be in that place.

G: Fasho that. Oooowe jive! Now I can help my mama and Lawrence plan the wedding. That's even better than just being there.

Darnell Jr.: On everything I'm happy your mama found true love. Cause your mama is a real good person, and she deserves somebody to love her.

G: For real and it's even better because Lawrence is a real solid dude. It's just blessings on top on blessings. I came in here and learned the lessons God was trying to teach me and took a few steps closer to being the man God wants me to be. Now I'm ready to be a free man!

Darnell Jr.: On everything, G! You'll feel even more free when you touch all this money we've racked up. See when you gotta get it out the mud, like us, life is only as good as your habits and only as powerful as your ambitions.

G: You wait until I come home. I'll show you ambition!

Darnell Jr.: I know that's right! I'm with you, brother'

G: When I come home, I want to start up a clothing line, Thoroughbred Threads. You know how I always wanted to be fresher than everybody and never wanted to dress like everybody else.

Darnell Jr.: Do I remember? Boy you've been like that since we were little kids. You remember that time Daddy took us to Flying Frogs and the movies and you had dressed all three of us?

G: *Laugh* Yeah I remember that. Y'all still dress like some country bumkins!

Darnell Jr.: *Laugh* Chill. That's a nice name too. Thoroughbred Threads.

G: Preciate that. I think that's what I'm supposed to do though. God gave me a talent so I'm going to utilize it.

Darnell Jr.: God works in mysterious ways for real. How bout I just met this girl in the clothing industry just yesterday! She gave me her business card and everything.

G: Fasho. Keep that. Soon as I get home, we are going to call her and see if she can help. I'm excited now. This phone is about to hang up though. Make sure you talk to the lawyer about Sanka for me big bruh.

Darnell Jr.: I got you too, brother. Don't worry about anything. I love you.

G: I love you too.

One week later: G is standing before the judge with the lawyer on his side. The arresting office is on the other side of the court. Quinita is seated on the plaintiff side. Darnell Jr., Darius, Darriah, Lil G, Cool-Pop, Tyree, Darnell, Takyia, Larry, Mama J., Mama Lee, Tellie, and Jamaica are all in the audience. Quinita's parents are not present. She didn't inform them because she didn't want them to know what she had done.

Sheriff: You may be seated.

Judge Bronston: Good morning. So Ms. Topple, it says here that you called 911 on March 19, 2015, reporting that Mr. Young physically abused you and then took off on foot, with drugs in his left pocket. Is that right Ms. Topple?

Quinita: That's what I reported, but...

Judge Bronston: A simple yes your honor or no your honor will do just fine.

Quinita: Yes, your honor.

Judge: Thank you. There was a piece of evidence that was submitted to the court. Let's take a listen.

After they watch the recording, everyone in the room is shocked. Then the Judge asked G to come to the stand to testify.

G: For God is my witness I'm about to tell you the truth. Quinita and I had broken up, but she was still carrying my son, so I went over to check on her from time to time. That night, when I walked into her house, she had a full glass of Circo, weed in her mouth, and some cocaine sitting on the table. I lost it. I started yelling and screaming because she was still eight months pregnant, with MY child. I slowly approached her, snatched the blunt and glass from her. I grabbed all the weed and cocaine she had on the table and put it in my left pocket. Instead of getting in my car to leave, I took a walk because I said some mean things and I knew I wanted to go back to apologize after I cooled down. But I never made it back.

Judge: You may return back to your seat, Mr. Young. Ms. Topple, how much of Mr. Young's story is true?

Quinita: All of it, your honor.

Judge: Then why did you lie? Why did you call the police in the first place, when all he did was try to prevent any birth defects, help you and your child, and tried to keep you from continuing to be a junkie? You realize what you've done? You took away your son's privilege of having a father in his life. You took a child away from his family. This young man was twenty years old serving time for a crime he didn't even commit because of you. With that being said, Mr. Young, you're a free man. I will completely erase this from your record and being that it's the only thing on your record, your slate is completely clean. I hope your future life is much better than the last four years.

G: Oh it will be. Thank you so much, your honor! Thank you! *smiling hard*

Judge: Court is adjourned.

Lil G: Daddy!

G: Lil G!

Lil G: *Run to G, jump and hug him* Daddy!

G: Ohhhh, big boy! Daddy missed you soooo much! I promise you, I will never leave your side again! *Cry* Mama!!

Keyawanna: Son!!!! *They hug for a long time.*

G: Mama J!!!

Mama J.: Keith!!!

G: I missed you, Mama J.

Mama J.: Oh my sweet baby! I missed you more!

G: I missed you too, Grandma Lee!

Mama Lee: You know I missed you, sugar foot! *kiss his cheek*

Darius and Darnell Jr.: Brother! *Hug G*

G: The D-Boys! Man I missed y'all so much!

Darius: They done let my brother outta jail. It's on now!

Darnell Jr.: It's up they and stuck they. On me, lil bruh!

G: Lil Ri, wassup!

Darriah: Brother!!!! *jump and hug G* I'm so glad you're home. It's a blessing! I swear!

G: Nothing but a blessing, Sister. I'm just ready to be the best father in the world *pick Lil G up*

Lil G: Daddy! Uncle Darius got a football field in his backyard. Come on so I can tackle you out there!

G: Lil G, you couldn't tackle me if you gave it all your strength.

Lil G: Oh I forgot you don't know me like that. I'm a strong boy!

G: *Bust out laugh* Ice cold, Lil G. Come on. Let's go!

*Darnell wraps his arm around G's neck and G is holding Lil G's head. Lil G is holding Darriah's hand.

The next day, everybody is in Darnell's backyard. Tables are filled with low country boils. Liquor is on another table. Speakers are blasting Darius' song, My Brother's Keeper.

Darnell: Boy, you came home just in time. We're about to get prepared for the program for young men. You are one of the best role models for them.

G: Yeah. I can't wait either. And my cellmate wants to be apart too. My lawyer is trying to getting him out of there. He already served forty-four out of sixty years. But he's really smart, and he definitely help mold me into the man I am today. I love the new G.

Darnell: You're supposed to love yourself. If you don't, you can't expect other people to love you. But when you love yourself and truly know who you are, you become untouchable. You know your worth and you know what you want and need, so you won't accept just anything from everybody.

G: That's true too. Guess what, Daddy. I'm getting ready to start a clothing line, Thoroughbred Threads.

Darnell: That's a nice name, but don't just talk about it. Be about it. So many people have excellent ideas, but never pursue them because they don't want to put in the required work.

G: And that's one way I'm different from others. When I ask God for something, I'm always ready to put in the work, because I know faith without work is dead. How do you ask God to make you the best of the best, but you never practice?

How do you expect to get better if you don't perfect your craft?

Darnell: Exactly, son. Well best of luck to you on that adventure. If you ever need me to model for you, you know where I'm at. *Stop and pose like a model*

G: *Laugh* Man, thank you, Daddy. *Walk away*

Darnell Jr.: G, you came home just in time! We getting major bread, and you can enjoy every penny. Lil bruh, you don't even know how much I missed you.

G: Oh, I know because I missed you just as much.

Darnell Jr.: I had called the girl about the clothing line. Her name is Jennifer. We set-up a business meeting for tomorrow at four pm. You have to get started immediately because you can't let anybody out work you.

G: Oh boy. Everything is so real. Like, I've seen all of this before living it. I consistently trust in God, and now I'm finally here! I'm excited for our future endeavors because we are not stopping here.

Darnell Jr.: Hell nah we not stopping here! It's plenty more life to live and I'm not stopping until I know what's beyond the sky.

G: You be thinking like that too?

Darnell Jr.: All us do. Darius, Daddy, Darriah, and Lil G. It's in the blood, G. I know we can make it as a family. We're the black Kardashians. All of their mother's kids know how to make millions.

G: *Laugh* You ain't lying.

Darriah: G!! * Walk up and hug him* I'm so glad you're home brother.

G: I'm glad to be home too, lil sis. So wassup? Darnell Jr. say you got the self-made millionaire mind too.

Darriah: Oh I do. Right now, I'm trying to create a car design. I want to create the flying car that can also be a boat. I named it the Mallane.

G: Damn, Sis. Where did you get the name from?

Darriah: I was driving and I was thinking, I only mind my own business and I always stay in my own lane. My middle name is Malai and I kept repeating "my lane, Malai, my lane, Malai" and just said Mallane and it stuck with me. So I ran with it. And I knew it was the right choice cause we got a cousin named Mellane.

Darnell Jr.: I told you, boy! It's a family thing!

G: *Laugh* Fasho that, Ri. How much is it going to cost you to build it? With the cost of production, do you think you are going to make a profit? Who are you targeting? Is it going to run off gas, is it a solar power car, or electric? What is your market price?

Darriah: I just came up with the idea the other day. I still have work to do, so save those questions in your mind. I will get back with you with the answers.

G: I like how you handled that with ease. Somebody else would have folded under the pressure.

Darriah: Pressure bust pipes, not me.

G and Darnell JR.: *Laugh* Well alright, lil sis. Do your thing!

Larry: *Standing alone, yell from the other side of the yard* G!

G: Let me go holla at him y'all. *Walk up to Larry* Wassup, Lawrence?

Larry: Say. I just wanted to ask you an important question.

G: What's on your mind?

Larry: You know, when I first saw you, I knew it was something special about you. Beyond you being the child of my only true love, you stood out. After getting to know you, you really grew on me. We built a bond that I've never had with anybody else. I truly feel like you are my own son and in less than a year, you will be my step-son. So I was wondering, if you would be my best man.

G: Aww man, you already know I will! *hug him* Growing up, I didn't have one father figure. Now I have multiple. I swear God is so good to me.

Larry: He's definitely good. My whole life, I always wanted a big family, but it was always only me and my Dad. Now Being surrounded by everybody here, all the love, I know my time is now. As soon as me and your mama get married, I'm going to take her on a few trips, then I'm going to impregnate her a couple times. I want some kids.

G: *Buss out laughing* Oh yeah! I'm all for it! Then Lil G could be the best nephew in the world.

Larry: Man. Lil G already acts like he is somebody daddy. I know how he gone treat them kids.

G: Boy, I ain't gone lie. You might as well gone head and get her pregnant like a few months right before the wedding. It takes nine months, if everything go right. That's plenty time to take trips.

Larry: You right too. What's the point of waiting for a long time anyway? We are already up there in age.

G: Y'all already had this discussion?

Larry: Yeah. She down for whenever. I just wanted to wait for a lil minute so I can enjoy my wife, because once you have kids, you should dedicate the majority, if not all of your time to them.

G: And I completely understand that. Well do what's in your best interest.

Larry: Mama J really wants some more grandkids right now. Ima take your advice and knock her up like two months before the wedding. That way, she won't be showing so much in her wedding dress and it'll give us ample time to travel.

G: Oh yeah. It's going down ni. They done blessed up letting a real man outta jail! I'm finna turn up ni!

Cheaters Never Prosper Daddy!: A Week Later

Lil G and G getting ready to play football in the backyard.

Lil G: I bet you I can put my shoes on faster than you Daddy!

G: Bet that up. On your mark, get set, go! *racing to put on shoes, Lil G moving extremely swift and mistakeless. G struggles to get the shoe on his feet because he tries to cheat by sliding it on while it's already tied.*

Lil G: Cheaters never prosper Daddy!

G: What you talking about? I didn't cheat.

Lil G: I won! And yeah, you tried to put the shoe on with it already being tied up. That's cheating!

G: *Laugh* You're right.

Lil G: Come on slowpoke. I bet you I can get to the field before you Daddy!

G: Everything is a competition with you. Come on. Now I know ima win this one.

Lil G: Alright. Don't cheat either. On your mark, get set, go! *take off running full speed*

G: *run slow behind Lil G* Dang you fast son!

Lil G: You better catch up.

G gets outside and scoops Lil G off his feet and puts him on his neck and runs to the field. He swings him in the air, around in a circle, real fast until they both get dizzy. Put him on his feet and watch him stumble then fall together at the same time.

Lil G: *laugh* Daddy the world is spinning!

G: *laugh* I know son. Guess what though. I see you like to compete, but you don't have to compete with other people. Compete with yourself.

Lil G: How am I supposed to compete by myself, Daddy? I can't race myself.

G: Oh, but you can, Lil G. You see, in life, your major goal is to be the best you that you can be. See because, I don't want you growing up thinking you're better than anybody. As long as you're only working on yourself, you'll always be okay. Let me show you how you can race yourself. Are you still dizzy?

Lil G: No sir.

G: Come on. Stand up. Okay, now I want you to run to the pond and come right back to me. *Pull phone from pocket and open the stopwatch* Get on your mark. *Lil G gets ready* Get set. Go! *Start Stopwatch.

He watches his son run to the pond and back. Lil G is running back, hold out hand so he can slap himself in and stop the clock.

Lil G: I'm fast, ain't it Daddy!?

G: You sure are, Lil G! This is your time. *He shows him the phone.* This is how you compete with yourself. As you do it again and again, this number should go down and that's how you know you're improving. If it goes up, you need to step your game up. When you're running track, this is how they time you. Yeah, you're running next to other people, but you're not racing them. You're racing the clock.

Lil G: So I have to practice everyday so that I can be the greatest!

G: Lil G. I want you to be the best version of yourself. Whatever you choose to do in life, always give it one thousand percent. Never try to take the easy way out because you'll never learn that way. Your greatest lessons always come through pain and failures. So don't try to avoid the storm because that's how you become strong. What doesn't kill you definitely makes you stronger and wiser. Always remember that, son. And the storm doesn't last always, so you have to have faith, patience, and a relationship with God. And I promise, you will always make it through, better than you were before. You understand?

Lil G: Yes sir!

G: Go get the ball. Let's run some drills.

The Next Morning, 5:30 am

G walks in Lil G's room, turns on the big light and blows a whistle.

G: What are you doing sleep? You're supposed to be training!

Lil G: Huh?

G: Yesterday you told me you wanna be a superstar football player. Superstars are always in training. So get up! I'm finna turn on this stopwatch. How fast can you: make your bed up, get dressed, brush your teeth, and make it to the kitchen table? Annnd GO! *Start watch and walk to the kitchen. Grab Lil G a banana and pour him a glass of water. Five minutes have passed, then ten, then fifteen. And Lil G come running down the stairs* You took up way too much time up there.

Lil G: I had to make up the bed and brush my teeth and...

G: Sounds like a bunch of excuses. In life, you either get reason or results. You want results. Today, you took fifteen minutes. Tomorrow, will your time be lower or higher?

Lil G: Lower.

G: Don't be all talk, Lil G. You gotta prove it. *Hand him banana* Here's your breakfast. Hurry up and eat. We got work to do.

Five minutes later, G and Lil G walk outside the back door seeing the backyard turned into an actual football field, with white lines, cones, ladders, and new cleats for Lil G. Lil G runs up to the cleats and screams.

Lil G: Thank you, Daddy! Now I'm finna be raw for real.

G: Listen, Lil G, you can look the part with the best gear, the flyest shoes, handband and all, but the shoes don't make you. It's what you do in the shoes that makes you. It's where you go in those shoes that makes you, Lil G. You get it, son?

Lil G: Yes sir!

G: Listen. I'm not finna stand over you and make you do something I wouldn't do. So we are going to be doing this together. Okay?

Lil G: Okay.

G: Okay. So we're gonna start off with two warm up laps around the field. Then we're gonna run through a few warm up drills: high knee, butt kicks, karaokes, squats, push ups, jump and jacks, and sit ups. After that, we're gonna work on speed for the rest of the day. Ready? Let's go. *Lil G takes off* Stop! Lil G. We are going to be exercising for at least two hours. You have to stretch your energy. Take your time and go at your own pace so you don't get tired so fast. Don't try to keep up with me either. Because my pace is not your pace. Remember, you are only competing with yourself.

Lil G: Yes sir.

Ace Hood Hustle Hard starts off the boy's exercising session for the next couple hours. The sky changes from dark blue to deep dark purple, to lavender and soft pink, then to red and blue, then solid blue with beautiful, white clouds. Lil G is going as hard as possible to impress his Daddy. G is going as hard as possible to set the best example for his son. They take water breaks and go hard again.

G: Got dang, boy! You were on fire today, son!

Lil G: Yeah because Ima hot boy, Daddy! I stay on fire!

G: * Buss out laughing* Where do you get that from?

Lil G: Uncle Cool-Pop always listening to the Hot Boyz, and I wanna be on fire like them boys, Daddy!

G: Fasho that Son, but guess what though. It's okay to be confident and all that, but you have to know what you're

227

capable of and still remain humble. Don't let your talents make you a conceited and arrogant man. Nobody likes cocky people. It's not attractive. You hear me?

Lil G: Yes sir.

G: Let your talents speak for you. Talk is cheap. Your actions define who you are.

Mindset and Ambition: Three days later

Lil G and G are in the Oglethorpe Mall. They're walking past a group of girls who are staring G right in the face, wearing a huge smile.

Lil G: Man, Daddy. Those girls are choosing.

G: *Laugh* Man, what do you know bout somebody choosing?

Lil G: Uncle DJ always say that the girls are choosing him and jive because they like to flirt and try to get with him to chose them back.

G: Yeah, you're Uncle DJ always had the girls all over him. But look son. It's not about how many girls you can get and all that. Cause some of these women don't have good intentions. Some of them just wanna use you for your money. Some of them just wanna use you for something else, that I'll tell you about when you're older. When you get old enough to date, always remember, looks are not everything. Just cause she is fine with a big butt and all that, don't make her the right woman to keep around.

Lil G: But Uncle Tyree said his girls always gotta be a dime piece, or she can't even come around.

G: *Laugh* Son, yeah everybody want somebody attractive, but looks is not the only thing that matters is what I'm saying. She has to have a decent head on her shoulders. She has to actually care about your well-being and not just your wallet. You need a woman to match your mindset and ambition, not your fly. You get it, Lil G?

Lll G: Yes sir. So you're saying, she can be fine, but she gotta be smart too. She can have a big butt, but she has to have a big brain to go with it. What kind of girls you like, Daddy?

G: I like women, Lil G. I'm too old for girls, but I like ambitious women, with goals and high expectations. I like women that care about how they look when they walk out the house. I like women that can throw down in the kitchen. I like women that can make me laugh.

Lil G: What about their skin color? You like dark or light skin women?

G: Listen, Lil G. Your skin color doesn't define who you are. You can't control what God gives you. I don't care if she's dark and lovely or light and bright, as long as she's black.

Lil G: You don't like white women?

G: They just aren't my preference. I'm all about black love. I need me a strong-minded black woman. I need me a woman like my mama. That's just what I prefer, that's all.

Lil G: Well when I get older, I want me a pretty, strong-minded, ambitious, independent, black woman too.

G: That's what I'm talking bout, son. But you gotta be strong to deal with her. A real woman deserves a real man. A loyal man that's not afraid of showing his love for her, even in front of your homeboys. A real man that will protect her in this cruel world. A real man that's financially stable to provide for her. Not asking for money and to use her for what she's got. Cause when you're in a relationship with a black woman, what's yours is hers and what's hers belongs to her. *Laugh* Hopefully you don't get a selfish woman. You understand? And You can like any race of women: white, black, Hispanic, whatever.? That's totally up to you.

Lil G: Yes sir.

G: Lil G, I'm just preparing you for the world. I just want you to be a better man than me. I want you to grow up with great morals and values. I want to teach you the things I wish my dad taught me at your age. I just wanna be there for you whenever you need me and even when you don't.

Lil G: Daddy, I asked Auntie Ri why you were locked up, but she told me to ask you when you got out. Did my mama lock you up, Daddy?

G: Oh boy. Well son. I will never, ever lie to you. Always remember that. Yes, son. You're mama set me up. You were still in your mama's stomach. I walked in her house and she was drinking alcohol and doing drugs that could have killed you. I was so upset that I was screaming and yelling at her. So I took all the drugs from her and I left. She lied to the police and told them I beat her up, and I was dealing drugs. Lil G, I never hit your mama or any woman, and I never will. I never sold drugs a day in my life, and I never will.

Lil G: That's evil, Daddy. Why would she do something so evil to us. You were locked up for that long time because she was being evil? I didn't get to see or touch you because she was being evil? Oh no. Now I'm mad, Daddy. Am I wrong? Can I be mad at my mama?

G: You have every right to be mad, son. But you know what? Pastor Morris says if you hold grudges, you won't have a free hand to catch your blessings. So now you know, but don't be mad or disrespectful to your mama. Everything happens for a reason. And I'm not happy I was away from you, but I'm proud of who I became while being in there.

Lil G: You're the best Daddy in the world. I'm glad you're my daddy. *hug and kiss G*

Essential Life Lessons: The next weekend

Darnell, Tellie, Mel, Quel, Cool-Pop, Tyree, Darnell Jr.,
Darius, G, Lil G, Larry, and Sanka are sitting in Darnell's
dining area.

Tellie: First, we find a building to hold our program.

Darnell Jr.: How often will we meet with the boys?

Tellie: Good question. How would y'all feel about one
Thursday, Friday, Saturday, and Sunday, every month?

Darnell: If we gone do it, then we gotta do it. I'm down. But
what about food? We have to feed them everyday.

Larry: How about we try to get a sponsorship with Publix,
Kroger, and Wal-mart. We convince them to donate food,
and we can find some good-hearted women to volunteer to
cook it for us.

Quel: That's a great idea. Well what about field trips? We
can't keep them in the building all day, everyday.

Mel: Well the real question is, where do we take them for
field trips. There's nothing for children to do in the
Savannah. It's a retirement city.

Tellie: You're right about that.

G: Well, we can take them bowling, skating, swimming, golfing, fishing, to museums, and to the park. That's all the stuff we use to do when we went to Camp Ashtree. Mr. Brown and his family made that the best summer camp I ever went to.

Darnell Jr.: They did for real. I use to be up super early, dressed and all. Ready to go to camp.

Darius: They had some real disciplinarians there though. Ms. Arnold used to check me everyday. But as I got older, I started to appreciate that. I appreciate her for keeping me in line and out of trouble.

Darnell: And that's how we have to treat these boys. Give me the tools they need to stay on the right track and turn them into successful men.

Mel: That's right. How about we take them out of the city sometimes. Dave and Busters, Six Flags, the aquarium, water parks, Universal Studios, college tours, Washington D.C.

Tellie: Man, this thing is about to be huge! We can bring in motivational speakers to talk to them.

G: I'm not gone front. I was in a program like this. It was called SLP, Student Leadership Program. We used to leave school for the whole day. We learned lessons that are essential to life. We had motivational speakers come talk to us. In the summer, we took trips. And we used to win prizes too.

Cool-Pop: What kind of prizes?

G: Everything really: gift cards to everywhere, movie passes with the big popcorn bucket filled with candy, bikes, headphones, money, all kinds of stuff.

Tyree: Everybody won?

G: Nah. We would put our names on a card and they would pull like five or more names each time we met up. But at the very end of senior year, everybody gets $250. Right before my senior year, they used to take all the seniors to New York.

Larry: New York!? Man I should have been a teacher to catch that free ride to New York!

Darnell Jr.: Ain't it!

Tellie: Now that's a great idea. I'm already excited about this because even though we're small now, we can grow into a program like that.

Mel: Me too. I just wish I had something like this when I was younger.

Sanka: Me too, but now we have the chance to be the mentors. There was a time where we were stuck in jail and couldn't be apart of anything but the chain gang. So I'm extremely thankful to be part of this with you guys. This is truly a blessing.

Darnell: That's right. God gave us all another chance to get it together. So let's make him proud and take advantage of these times. We are about to start a brand new life. We are about to be the cause of better for these young men. We are about to be role models. Lil G, you're the present and the future. We need you to pay close attention to everything that's about to happen because you have to continue our legacy. We're about to change the world.

Tellie: We have to find Ty and Torrance. They're the first ones out of our group to invest their drug money into their own business.

G: They still have their lawn care service. My mama still does business with them.

Larry: I'll call her. What's going on, Keya. I'm in this meeting with the men, and they wanted to know if you still have Ty and Torrance's number. Yeah baby, I'm ready. 912- 555-8899.

Alright baby. Thank you. I'll talk to you later. I love you too.

Tellie: Hello. May I speak to Ty or Torrance. This is Tellie.

put the phone on speaker

Torrance: I know this not Tellie Tell!

Ty: Tellie, wassup boy!?

Tellie: How y'all boys living?

Torrance: Look here Tellie. We are living the good life.

Wassup with you? I see your label blew up to the top.

Tellie: Yeah. God is real good to us. Listen, me, Darnell, Mel,

Quel, And a whole lot of other men are starting a new

program to better guide the young men in the city. How

about you guys come join us? We are going to go global with

this right here.

Ty: Say less. Man, we are always down to give back to the

community.

Tellie: Fasho! Okay so meet us at Darnell's house tomorrow

at four pm. I'll text you the address. We are having another

informational meeting for all the men volunteering their

time to help these young men.

Three months later, Tellie and Darnell are in the car, riding on their old block, reminiscing about the old time.

Darnell: Say cuz, do you remember that day Sho You Right came up and was dancing like his legs were on fire. That was hilarious!

Tellie: I swear we were dying laughing! But when that man started singing, I had to put all jokes aside. You remember that day when Juju was on the percs the doctor prescribed him, and he had messed around and was smoking all that weed with us?

Darnell: Do I remember!? How could I forget!? That boy Juju was tweaking so hard! *dying laughing* He kept laughing at everything moving.

Tellie: Boy that could have killed me when he called Pizza hut, ordered the food then tried to pay with the food stamp card!

Darnell: They kept talking bout "Sir it's declining. Is it a visa or mastercard? He talking bout "Girl this is the card from Master Government! Come one, girl! Just hook your boy up! My stomach as empty as your head." Man you remember when we were fifteen, standing right in front of this store, tryna convince the OGs to put us on?

Tellie: How could I forget the brokest time of my life. We were so broke, we had weed but didn't have a dollar for the blunt, and we turned an apple into a bong.

Darnell: Mannn I almost forgot about that! Desperate times calls for desperate measures. You remember that time when we were like ten. We were at my auntie's house starving, and she sent us to the store? But we couldn't remember the PIN number, and we didn't know her phone number so we had to walk back.

Tellie: Nah, Darnell. We walked back and forth three times! And that wasn't a quick walk. That was at least a mile. Tell me why nobody thought to write the pin down?

Darnell: The worst part was that we swiped the card so many times, that when we remembered the password, her card was blocked until the next day. *Buss out laughing* Bruh we hated each other that day.

Tellie: Auntie Tiese tore us up that day too. *Pull up to liquor store* Come in here with me right quick.

They're walking down the brown liquor aisle. Tellie is looking one way, while Darnell is focused on the drinks.

Tellie: Why does that girl look so familiar? Where do I know her from? D, look man. I don't know why she looks so familiar.

Darnell: *Look up* Because that's Brionna, cuz.

Tellie: Brionna who?

Darnell: Darius' mama. I wonder when she got out.

Tellie: Nooo, sure is!! Wow! I completely forgot all about that time she tried to kill Takyia.

Darnell: Man, I'ma go holla at her. *Walk up to Brionna* Wassup? When they let you out Ms. Bout it Bout it?

Brionna: I thought sure somebody would have killed you by now.

Darnell: *Laugh* Get outta here. When did you get out?

Brionna: Last year.

Darnell: Twenty years in prison. Dang, Brionna. How are you doing?

Brionna: How does it look like I'm doing?

Darnell: Listen. I know you done been through some hard times. I know prison is nowhere anybody wants to be.

Especially for no dark twenty years. But what goes around never forgets to swing right back around.

Brionna: Darnell, what do your funky tail want?

Darnell: All that time in prison. You come home in just enough time to get your life together, but *Take big bottle of liquor out her basket* you still choose to make bad decisions.

Brionna: First of all, you don't know me. Don't come round here trying to judge me like you got it so all together. You don't know what I've been through. You don't know my life.

Darnell: Brionna, it's 2019. Times have truly changed. If you don't like something, change it! You're not in prison anymore. You have every right to change for the better. You have like five or six kids out here wishing their mother was in their life. You just gone drink your life away to an early grave, instead of making it right with your kids?

Brionna: Them kids don't care if I'm dead or alive, Darnell. And I don't know if they are either.

Darnell: Look at how you treated them, Brionna! But like I said, times have changed and it's never too late to get your life on the right track. Where are you staying right now?

Brionna: I'm homeless, Darnell. Nobody wants to hire an attempted murderer, so I don't have any money to buy a house. The projects won't even let me get a place.

Darnell: I have a place I can let you live, but under one condition.

Brionna: What's that?

Darnell: You have to change, Brionna. You have to change your perspective on life. You have to change your habits. You have to change your mindset. You have got to get a relationship with the Lord. But you have to have a whole lot of patience and will power. Once you're all better, you can get back into your kids' lives and be the mother that they need. It's never too late until you're dead. Put the bottles back. I'll take you to the grocery store, then you can go home.

Brionna: Darnell, thank you! Thank you so much!

Later that evening. Takyia is in the kitchen cooking. Darnell walks in the house.

Darnell: Takyia! Takyia, where are you at!?

Takyia: What is he yelling for. I'm in the kitchen!

Darnell: *Walk in kitchen* Baby! You'll never guess who I ran into today.

Takyia: I'm not tryna guess either. Who?

Darnell: Brionna. Darius' mama!

Takyia: What! When did she get out of jail?

Darnell: Last year, some time. I mean, she looked awful.

Takyia: What do you expect for somebody that has been rotting in prison for the past twenty years?

Darnell: Right, but she said she was homeless. Nobody would hire her. She had nobody to call on. I had to do something. So I let her stay in the old house on 42nd.

Takyia: You did what!?

Darnell: What are you yelling for?

Takyia: The same woman that tried to kill me!? The same person that totalled your car!? That same person that treated your son, her own blood son like a stray dog! That's the same person you gave a house to, Darnell? That same person ?

Darnell: The bible tells you to love your enemy. Treat them just as you want to be treated. Too much time has passed for

244

me to still be holding grudges and hating people. Hating only corrupts your soul and hinders your blessings. I had to ask myself, what would God do in this situation? So I did what I did out of the kindness of my heart. If you can't find it in your heart to forgive, even after God spared your life, then you need to ask God to help you.

Takyia: Darnell, I want a divorce.

Darnell: What do you mean you want a divorce!? Because I'm trying to change my life around and become the person God wants me to be? You gone leave me because I'm helping out the mother of my child in her time of need?

Takyia: No, Darnell. I'm leaving you because I don't love you anymore. I haven't been happy since Darriah was one year old. Right before you left for those twelve years. While you were gone, I was depressed. I was lonely. I was even suicidal. You never once asked how I am doing? You never once asked if I'm okay. You never once asked how I feel about something. Everything was and still is all about what Darnell wants and needs. I never even stopped to consider my own happiness. Well guess what, Darnell. It's 2019. I want a divorce. I want to get to know myself. I want to know what it's like to be selfish. I want to know what it's like to genuinely be happy, Darnell. And I won't find out living here with you. So I'm leaving. My child is grown. I have my own money, so I don't need anything from you. I've already found me a house in Africa. So you can have this one. Goodbye, Darnell. *Walk off*

Darnell: *grabs her arm, and gets on his knees* Baby please! I can change! I need you! I care about you, Takyia. I do! Please don't do this to me! Please!

Takyia: Darnell, get up. I don't love you. *snatch arm and leave*

Darnell: *Scream cry* Why did you stay so long?

Takyia: Because I cared about your feelings more than my own. I didn't want to leave you while you were down. I would feel terrible, but since you're straight now, I'm good to go.

The next day:

Darnell in the bedroom, listening to Atlantic Starr- If Your Heart Isn't In It, crying like a baby, heartache written all over his face.

A week later:

Darnell, Tellie, Mel, Quel, Ty, and Torrance are sitting in Darnell's living room.

Darnell: She said I was selfish, careless, and she doesn't love me anymore.

Tellie: That's messed up. Well why did she not leave sooner. Like why would she leave now?

Darnell: She said she didn't want to leave me while I was down, in jail and when I came home and didn't have too much of nothing. Then on top of everything, she said she's moving to Africa.

Everybody: Africa!

Quel: I can't even lie. I would move to Africa too if I was trying to get away from everybody and find myself .

Mel: The farthest I'll go is Hawaii. I feel like, with the president y'all got in office, if I leave, I don't know if they'll let me back in this country

Ty: This man talking about "with the president "y'all" got. He's more your president than mine because you don't wanna leave, but I'll pick up and leave this country and never look back. I'm not going to because this is where my family is.

Quel: You know what'll be funny. If we all pack up our entire families and move to Africa, in the same country as Takyia.

Everybody: *Laugh*

Tellie: Boy, she'll be so mad!

Ty: I ain't gone hold it. That's pretty much what happened in Pooler. A couple of folks moved up there and now the whole city up there.

Torrance: On everything! Walk outside and your old neighbor is speaking to you. You be like dang! I was tryna get away from you!

Mel: Then they put the outlet out there and everything else. Now the whole city stays in Pooler. *Doorbell* Who is that?

Tellie: I'll go see. *Walk to the door, open door*

Mama Lee: Tellie!!!

Tellie: Mama Lee!! How are you doing!? *Hug her*

Mama Lee: Aw baby, I'm doing just fine, by the help of the Lord. How have you been?

Tellie: I'm maintaining. Come on. Everybody's in the living room.

Mama Lee: *Walk in living room* Oh my sweet baby.

Darnell: Mama! *jump up and hug her and cry*

Mama Lee: I know it hurts. Let it out. It's okay.

Darnell: Mama, how could she do me like this?

Mama Lee: Darnell, listen. I know you probably aren't going to understand this, but just hear me. She wasn't happy. She hasn't been happy for a while. Sometimes in life, we tend to get comfortable with the life we're living and don't realize we aren't living up to our full potential. We know it's more to life than where we are now, and we actually want it. We want better for ourselves. So even if that means we have to hurt a few people in the process, we're going to get what we want, by any means necessary. That's how Takyia was feeling. She just found the courage to actually take action.

Darnell: I just wish I would have known I wasn't making her happy.

Mama Lee: Darnell, some women try to hide their emotions from the ones they love the most because they want to ensure their happiness. They care about everybody else's feelings but their own. Sometimes they actually do show signs, but if you aren't paying close enough attention, then you'll miss it.

Darnell: Mama, I'm hurting.

Mama Lee: Darnell, you're gonna hurt. That's the heartache you're feeling, but just trust your mama. In due time, you'll feel better and you'll realize it was for the better. Sometimes God takes away things that we depend on too much because He wants you to open your eyes and realize you can't depend on anybody in this world, other than Him. Sometimes, He takes things from you because He wants to replace it with something much better. Sometimes, He just wants to teach you a lesson. Talk to Him. I promise, He'll reveal the answer to you.

Darnell: Mama, I think the only thing that'll make me feel better right now is your special seafood gumbo and your peach cobbler with your praline ice cream.

Mama Lee: Anything for my baby. I'm going to the store. I'll be right back. *get up and leave*

Darnell: Thank you, Mama!

Torrance: What? I can't even get my mama to make me a sandwich.

Tellie: Ooooo, Darnell! You're clutch for that bruh! One thing I'll never forget, is that your mama be throwing down in that kitchen! Remember in middle school, when all us had slept over to your house, and your mama made that strawberry cheesecake ice and those sugar cookies from scratch!

Ty: I remember that! I'll never forget that. Those cookies were bussing!

I Want A Husband: One month later

Brenda is in the mall, on the phone with Darnell Jr.

Brenda: Darnell Jr., what do you want for your birthday?

Darnell Jr.: Mama, I need a wife. That's all I want for my birthday. I have everything I could ever want and need except love.

Brenda: Aww, Darnell Jr. Mama gone find you a good wife. Somebody to: take good care of you, care about your feelings, cater to you, cook and clean and never smell like onion rings.

Darnell Jr.: Alright, Lil Phat, but make sure she is pretty. But she gotta have a big butt. If her butt not big, don't bring her around me.

Brenda: Darnell Jr., please.

Darnell Jr.: I'm serious ni. How are you doing though, Mama?

Brenda: I'm doing just fine. I'm a little lonely now though.

Darnell Jr.: You want me to get you a dog?

Brenda: No, Son. I can't do anything with no dog. I want a husband or at least a good friend. Somebody I can talk to and hang out with.

Darnell Jr.: Well, you know my daddy's single now. I don't know. Maybe y'all can be friends.

Brenda: What do you mean single, Darnell Jr.!?

Darnell Jr.: Mama, Takyia told him she wanted a divorce one day last month. The very next day, she was in Africa.

Brenda: Whaaaaat!? She just up and left!? Right on, girl! She had to be just completely fed up! Oh my gosh! Africa!? *Buss out laughing* Well I be.

Darnell Jr.: *laugh* Oh yeah. She was fed up alright. But yeah. He probably needs a friend anyway. He doesn't need a relationship, but it's probably not healthy for him to be completely alone either. Plus, he doesn't trust anybody, and being that at one point, he trusted you to mother his child, your friendship would truly be appreciated.

Brenda: I don't know about all that, Darnell Jr.

Darnell Jr.: Mama don't be so quick to say no. Actually think about it. You'll be helping out somebody in need, while also meeting your needs. I'm not asking you to married the man, Mama. I'm just suggesting that a friendship would probably be a great idea. Plus, he's literally a changed man. He decided that he wanted to better himself, and he did it. He has a relationship with God. He's been working on becoming a better father. He's been working on becoming the best him that he could be. I see the progress and I'm actually very proud of him.

Brenda: Well, I guess I can call him, to see how he's doing. I'm in this mall. I'll call you later.

Darnell Jr.: Alright, Mama. I love you.

Brenda: I love you too, Darnell Jr. Y'all please be safe. It's getting crazier and crazier. Somebody getting kilt everyday, seems like.

Darnell Jr.: For real. I got you, Mama. You be safe too.

Brenda: Alright.

She hangs up the phone, and is talking out loud to herself.

Child she finally opened her eyes and realized she matters too. I'm proud of her. Hmm...maybe I should give him a call. *Picks up the phone* Child please. Who am I kidding? We wouldn't get along. *suck teeth* Darnell Jr's right. I shouldn't be so closed minded. Let me call this man. Hello. Hey, Darnell. How are you doing? Oh I'm good, thanks. I was just calling to see how you were doing. I heard about what happened. Yeah, I know too. Well I was thinking, maybe we could go get something to eat or go to a bar or something, you know? Whenever you're available. Okay, well how's tonight? That's good? Okay then, tonight at six, meet me at the River House on River Street. Alright see you then.

It is 6:05 p.m. and Darnell and Brenda are sitting down at the River House, smiling at each other.

Darnell: So Brenda, how have you been? I haven't seen or heard from you in a long time.

Brenda: You know, Darnell, I've been doing exceptionally well for myself. I've started a cleaning business, Scrubbing Bubbles. My clientele are big corporation businesses. I have whole neighborhoods, a good bit of houses in South Bridge and The Landings. Business is great, but my personal life is dull. I'm bored. I'm lonely. I have all this money with no one to enjoy it with. When you don't have love, your life is incomplete.

Darnell: That's a fact. I'm glad to hear about your business. But you know what I was thinking the other day?

Brenda: What's that?

Darnell: I want to buy an RV and travel the States.

Brenda: Darnell, shut up!

Darnell: No. I'm being serious.

Brenda: No, Darnell. I literally just went to price a RV, but I didn't get it because I didn't have anybody to fulfill my dream with.

Darnell: How much do they cost?

Brenda: The one that I fell in love with is $145,000. It's nice Darnell. It has a kitchen, and you can fit an extra long twin size bunk bed on it. It's in Tampa, Florida. So the plan was to take a flight down there, travel Florida, then just drive north, then go west.

Once I get to California, ima leave the RV and take a boat over to Hawaii for a spell. Then ima make my way back east.

Darnell: We, Brenda. We're going to make our way back east. When are we leaving?

Brenda: *Smile hard* For real, Darnell?

Darnell: Brenda, life is too short to be stagnant and dormant. I want to be full of life and go out with a bang. Ain't no telling when my last day is, so why sit by the house phone waiting for death to call? Why not run the country and let death catch me if it can.

Brenda: Darnell, that's a great way to look at life. I'm ready whenever you are.

Darnell: How about we leave tomorrow? We catch the flight, take an Uber to the RV and just leave. Why wait?

Brenda: You know what, Darnell, I'm down! Let's make it happen. Shoot. You only live once.

Chef Londonaire: A week later

Lil G and G are walking down River Street, on the river side. Lil G has on a yellow and blue striped collared shirt with khaki cargo shorts. G has on a white with red, blue, and green striped Polo shirt with army green cargo shorts.

G: This is the Savannah River, Lil G.

Lil G: Daddy, I want my own river. Really, Daddy, I want a bunch of water. I want some rivers, some oceans, some lakes, annnnd, I want a waterfall.

G: What are you gonna do with so much water?

Lil G: I just want a place where the fishes can live in pcace. Like nobody can fish in my water,Daddy. I want my water to be extra clean and super blue.

G: That's a good idea. What made you think of that?

Lil G: The other day, I was watching Animal Planet, and they said that the sea animals were in danger because people were littering and sometimes it kills the animals. I don't want the animals to die from our careless attitudes toward the planet.

G: *Smile* You are so intelligent. We have to get you your water then.

Lil G: Thank you, Daddy. Daddy, did you know that a female lion reaches her adult size by the time she's two years old!?

G: Nooo. I didn't know that son. That's interesting!

Lil G: I wish I was a lion. I'll be the king of the whole world, Daddy!

G: What would I be?

Lil G: You can be a king too. See, I'll have my own land and you'll have your own land. Then that way, we both can be kings.

G: I'm so thankful God blessed me with you. I swear, you're the best thing that has ever happened to me.

Lil G: I love you, Daddy.

G: I love you too, Lil G.

An extremely beautiful, dark skin, twenty-one year old, British girl is walking toward G. She is wearing some royal purple jeans, a brand new, white button down shirt with an abundance of gold jewelry on.

Layla: *Thick, British accent* Excuse me. Are you from here?

G: Yes. Can I help you?

Layla: Yes. I am looking for the absolute best place to dine in for dinner. I was told River Street is the place to be, but there are too many choices for me to choose.

G: To be honest with you? I don't eat down here. This is what the locals call "the tourist trap". So I wouldn't be able to answer your question.

Layla: Well, where would you recommend Mr...

G: G. My name is Keith, but everyone calls me G. And your name?

Layla: Layla.

G: Very nice to meet you. Well, it depends on what type of food you're looking for Layla.

Layla: To be completely honest with you, G, I'm looking for the absolute best food Savannah has to offer. I'm extremely hungry and I don't want to be disappointed.

G: Well, Ms. Layla, I know a lady named Chef Londonaire, that will give you exactly what you're looking for. She'll deliver it to wherever you are. How about this. You let me show you around my city, and I'll order all three of us some food. How does that sound?

Layla: I'm in. So who is this handsome young man?

Lil G: My name is King Kenneth, but everyone calls me Lil G. You're the most beautiful lady I've ever seen.

Layla: *Laugh* Well it is very nice to meet you, Young King. I truly appreciate your compliment.

G: Well umm, come on. Let's go for a walk.

G was astonished by Layla calling Lil G young king, being that is what Sanka calls him. G picks up the phone to call Londonaire.

G: Chef! Hey. How are you doing? Good. Listen. I'm downtown right now, and there's a beautiful young lady who came to Savannah, all the way from England, looking for the best food Savannah can offer. So I was wondering if you'd be able to bring us three plates of your best dishes . *to Layla* Are you allergic to anything?

Layla: No.

G: Nah, Londonaire. So whatever you bring is fine. You know I'm not picky. But listen, bring some desserts too. Yeah, you can just meet me in City Market, in the square. Alright. Shoot alright, sounds good. See you then. *hangs up the phone* She said she'll be here in fifteen minutes.

Layla: Fantastic!

G: In the meantime, *picks up the phone* Hello. May I get a pedicab for three. I'm located at the Hyatt. My name is G. Alright. See you soon. Come on. We gotta go up.

As soon as they get off the elevator, the pedicab is outside waiting

G: Yoo! Are you looking for G?

Cab driver: Yeah, man.

G: That's me. You get on first, Layla. *He helps her up.* Come on, Lil G. *He picks him up, then gets on* Our final destination is City Market, but we want to take the scenic route please. We need to waste fifteen minutes.

Cab driver: Heard that. So are you guys from here?

G: My son and I are, but the pretty lady isn't.

Layla: I am from Manchester, England.

Cab driver: Oh really? What brings you to Savannah?

Layla: Well I'm actually looking into attending SCAD in the fall. So I came to visit, to see if this is a city I'd like to settle in for a while.

Cab driver: I'm from New York, and I'll say this city is definitely worth the stay. I attend SCAD already. I'm majoring in graphic design.

Layla: How lovely. I'm interested in majoring in fashion marketing and management.

G: Oh interesting! I'm in the process of creating my own men's clothing line right now, Thoroughbred Threads.

Layla: How intriguing, Keith! That's a really nice name as well. So how far have you gotten?

G: Well, I'm a little over three months in. I've created a logo. I got everything trademarked. I've come up with the designs of all the clothes for every season. I've found a factory that I trust to make everything for me, for an extremely reasonable price too. I've found a building. Only thing I'm waiting on now is the clothes to be finished.

Layla: So you've invested a lot of money into this. So, how do you know it'll sell?

G: It's all about taking a risk. If you never play chance, you could never win. But it's all about the advertising as well. And, I have a huge support system, who knows somebody, who knows somebody else. So I'm plugged in from all sorts of directions. With that being said, I am highly confident that my brand will be a success.

Layla: I love your confidence.

Lil G: Me too, Daddy. Keep that up. I like that.

They pull up to City Market, and G's phone rings. He gives the phone to Lil G and tells him to answer it, so that he can focus on paying the cab driver.

Lil G: Hello? Oh hey, Auntie London. Yes ma'am, we're over here in the middle. Are you driving your truck? Oh I see you now. You see me yet?

Chef Londonaire pulls up in the Garlisha food truck. She parks right in front of Sorry Charlie's. She gets out of the truck and G, Layla, and Lil G meet her half way.

Londonaire: Hey, y'all! How are you doing tonight?

Everybody: Good and you?

Londonaire: I'm great. Thanks!

` She sits two bags on the table.

So I bought three different meals. One box has seafood rolls.

Open all three boxes.

The second box is the Sea platter box, with fried whiting, shrimp, oysters, and homemade fries. And the last one has spicy garlic honey glazed grilled salmon and shrimp, with sautéed squash, cream spinach and mashed potatoes.

For dessert, there is one peach cobbler, with butter pecan ice cream, one freshly baked, key lime cake, and one slice of fruit tart. I also bought three of my Frujiga juices.

Here Lil G. I know you like the peach mango flavor. G, I brought you the orange pineapple, and this is everyone's favorite, the strawberry Frujiga juice, for you Ms. Layla.

Layla: Oh my goodness! Everything looks and sounds terrifically amazing Londonaire! I must admit, I am thoroughly impressed!

G: No surprise, but she never ceases to impress me. Thank you, L'aire. You're truly appreciated. Here. You can keep the rest.

Londonaire: Thank you, G! Lil G, wassup!?

Lil G: Wassup, Auntie London!

Layla: Oh. G, is this your sister?

G: Nah. Layla. All the kids call her Auntie London.

Londonaire: So, Layla, what brings you all the way from England?

Layla: I was thinking about going to SCAD.

Londonaire: Awww, interesting. You'll love it. I promise! *phone ring* Ooph. Food lovers are calling, gotta go. I hope you all enjoy everything!*She answers the phone while walking off.* Soul Stove!

Layla: Ohhh, everything smells so great!

Lil G: I want the seafood rolls Daddy.

G: Alright. Which one do you want, Layla?

Layla: I'll take the salmon. She made it sound so tastebud pleasing. Oh, and I want the fruit tart. If that's okay.

G: Not a problem.

      Everybody starts to eat.

Layla: *Scream* Ahhhh! This is delicious!!! I've never had anything like this, in my life!

Lil G and G: *Buss out laughing*

      After they finish eating, they get up and take a walk down Broughton Street.

G: So Layla, tell me a little about you.

Layla: Well, I'm twenty-one, from the west side of Manchester, England. I was raised by my grandmother. My mother died after giving birth to me, and I don't know my father. I grew up loving art, music, and fashion. My birthday is September 9, 1997. Oh, and my last name is Patterson. Tell me about yourself.

G: My name is Keith Young. I turn twenty-five on June seventh. I grew up super close with my two brothers, one sister, my mama, and grandma. I'm the only child on my mama's side.

My dad was in prison the majority of my life, but we are building a relationship now. I just spent my last four years in prison, for trying to save my son's life. That was his whole life. So that's why I try to spend every moment with him. That's about it.

Layla: Well, Keith, I'll be returning to England in the next two days. So if it's okay with you, I'd definitely love to spend more time with you and your son.

Lil G: We'll love that!

G: *laugh.* We'll definitely be looking forward to the next two days, Layla.

Layla: Great!

The next day, Lil G is spending the day with his grandparents, Larry and Keya. So, G goes to pick Layla up from the Doubletree hotel on the corner of MLK and Bay Street. He takes her to Forsyth Park and calls Londonaire for some breakfast. London brings them one seafood omelettes, which contains: shrimp, crab meat, and salmon with bell peppers, spinach, onion, and lots of cheese. It also comes with one bowl of grits.

The other plate is her infamous smothered shrimp and grits. She serves it with two freshly squeezed orange juices. After breakfast, they take a walk around the park and get to know each other a little better. G finds out that Layla is a LeBron James fan, just like him. They make arrangements for her to come back to the States just so they can attend a Lakers game together. For the rest of the day, they go to the movies to see Londonaire's Land of the Truth, to the mall for a spell, and they finish the night with a long walk, around Daffin Park, under a beautiful starry sky. The weather is completely dry. There's no wind, no heat, just a smooth seventy-five degree Fahrenheit night. It's beautiful.

Layla: G. There's a sparkle in your left eye. Did you know that?

G: Nah, tell me bout it.

Layla: Well, it's like there's a star just swimming in the deep end of your eye. There's something special about you, G. I just can't put my finger on it. You have a magnetic soul that attracted me to you, and now I don't want to let it go.

G: You don't have to. Layla, You have my full attention. You bring a joy to my spirit that not even Lil G has reached. It's a different type of feeling you give me though. I know what it is. I just don't wanna scare you away or anything Layla, but it's the truth.

Layla: What is it, Keith?

G: Love at first sight. Do you believe in it?

Layla: G, I didn't randomly choose you to guide me to a nice restaurant. I saw you and I decided to make the first move, very discreetly. I didn't want to go back to England without getting to know you first. So yes, I do believe in it.

G: *big smile* Wow. So this is destiny. You know, I don't even live here. I only came down for the weekend, because my mama wanted to spend time with Lil G.

Layla: *bigger smile, blush* Wow, Keith. I thought this only happens in movies.

G: My life is a movie. Now that you're apart of it, I want to give you a very important lead role, if you think you can act the part.

Layla: *still smiling* And what role would that be?

G: Be my lady. Listen, I know we've just met. I know you don't know me all that well. I know this, but Layla, you sparked a fire in me that I didn't even know existed. This entire day has been like living in a fantasy that I pray I can stay forever. I don't want it to end, Layla.

Layla: Yes.

G: Yes?

Layla: Yes, G. I'll be your lady. Whatever you want me to do, I'll do it.

G: Layla, I live in Atlanta. It's about four hours away from here. If you think SCAD is the school for you, come to the one in Atlanta. There are more opportunities there anyway. You'll save a lot of money too because you don't have to live on campus.

Layla: Okay, G. I'll come.

G: *Big smile* When does the semester start?

Layla: September.

G: Aw, come on. That's a minute away.

Layla: Well I can sign up for summer courses.

G: Now that's more reasonable. So how are we going to do this? You want me to come to England to meet your grandmother or you wanna bring her here, and we can meet each other's families all at once. Or what do you want to do?

Layla: Actually. My grandmother died a few months ago. I don't have any other family. It's just me. I live a rather lonely life there.

G: Well lucky for you, I have a humongous family. You'll be surrounded by love. My mama, Keyawanna, is about to get married to a man named Larry and he's just like you. He doesn't have much family. He grew up with his dad and now he's dead. And now he's joining our family. God is definitely using my entire family, and I'm loving it.

Layla: Oh, Keith. You're so amazing.

G: *Smirk* Thanks. So listen. I think, if you're okay with rushing things, you should come on to Atlanta with me and

Lil G. He'll love that. He asked me last night if I was going to marry you.

Layla: * Laugh* Really?

G: Yeah. I was like, Lil G, you don't typically marry somebody you just met, but now I know. He knew something that I didn't.

Layla: Yeah. He's extremely intelligent, Keith. He's going to go very far in life. But, I would love to move there with you.

G: I know this is all happening so quickly, and I don't want to scare you. So my uncle has a house in Atlanta that he rents out. You can stay there. I know you don't know me, so I don't want to force you to move in with me all fast like that. You know?

Layla: I'm definitely down, G.

G: *Laugh* Fasho that. Well come on. I'll take you back to your hotel.

I Saw The Whole Thing: The Next Day

The next day, Quinita is sitting on the porch, on the phone with her mother, on speaker phone.

Quinita: What y'all doing over there, mama?

Mrs. Topple: Nothing, child. Just sitting here looking at your daddy's old ugly face.

Mr. Topple: Who you calling ugly, you old hag.

Mrs. Topple: Who are you calling an old hag? You old, I need an iron to my old wrinkled face, looking boy.

Mr. Topple: Girl, I know you better be the last one to call somebody old. You've been old since 1973. You better go check the mailbox to see if Jurassic Park sent you your check for playing the dinosaur in the movie.

Mrs. Topple: Shut your stinking mouth, you old Harpo. I see your eyes are still black from when I jabbed you the other day.

Quinita: Mama, you been beating on him?

Mrs. Topple: Girl I've been in control of this marriage since the first day. He knows who wears the pants around here.

Quinita: Mama, that's not healthy.

Mrs. Topple: Girl, mind your business. How are you doing anyway? And where is Kenneth?

Quinita: Kenneth is supposed to be coming over here shortly. I'm doing fine.

Mrs. Topple: What is shortly? So I can make my way over there? I haven't seen my grandbaby in a very long time. You let that boy move my baby all the way to Atlanta. I'm not okay with that!

Quinita: I mean, the man wants his son with him. And quite frankly, I can use the break. Shoot, Lil G is sickening anyway. He always wanna talk my head off about animals and all that. Then he thinks he knows everything. I'm glad he is with his daddy.

Mrs. Topple: Yeah. That's probably the best place for him.

A young black boy comes flying around the corner, running right in front of Quinita's porch. Three policemen are running about three feet behind him. The boy slows down and yells.

Shawn: I can't breathe! I can't breathe! I surrender! I can't breathe!

The police let bullets fly. The boy tries to run, a bullet catches his leg. He's still hopping trying to get away. He's dragging his leg, running closer and closer toward Quinita. A police car comes flying down the street with his sirens screaming loudly in their ears.

Mrs. Topple: Quinita! What the hell is going on round there.

The young, white, police jumps out of his car and lets the entire magazine loose. A bullet hits Quinita in the forehead and another bullet hits the boy in the back of the head. The officer is still shooting. He hits Quinita in the left eye. He hit Shawn three more times in the back, and he hit Quinita once more in the chest.

Mrs. Topple: Quinita! Quinita! Oh lord!! Not my baby, Lord! James, let's go! Let's go!

G pulls up and sees all the police surrounding Quinita's project house.

G: What the hell is going on!? *gets out the car* Lil G, stay in the car! *walking up to the scene* WHAT IN THE WORLD!

Police: Sir, back up!

G: That's my son's mother laying there dead! Don't tell me to back up!

Lil G comes running up to G.

Lil G: Daddy!!!

G: G, please get back in the car.

Lil G: Daddy is that mommy?

G: Lil G, please son. Get back in the car.

Lil G: *Wrap around G's leg and cry hysterically*

G: WHAT IN THE WORLD HAPPENED!?

Old lady #2: I saw the whole thing. And my grandbaby recorded it on his cellular phone. So tell him the truth.

Police: It was an accident.

Old lady #2: Accident nothing. Ain't nobody shoots somebody twenty times by accident. Don't worry. I got all the evidence I need to get your lying self convicted. Don't you worry, young man. They're going to get justice. I got all the evidence. Accident nothing. Y'all police make me sick to my stomach. You're just a big ole gang. Don't worry. I got all the evidence I need. I need an Alka-Seltzer. Y'all make my stomach churn. You sick bastards. Baby, run cross that street and bring grandmama a glass of water and a pack of

Alka-Seltzer. I'm staying right here til the news peoples come. Cause I saw the whole thing, and so did my camera. You's a dirty bastard. God knows what you did, and you will pay for it. I saw the whole thing.

Mister and Mrs. Topple pull up and the second she gets out of the car, she begins to scream.

Mrs. Topple: Noooooooooo!!!!!! Not my baby Lord! Why Lord! Pleaseeeeee! Nooooo!!!! *grab hold off Quinita's body* Lord whhhhhhhy!!!!!!?

Mr. Topple: *falls to his knees and cry aloud*

WTOC's camera crew shows up on the scene.

Old lady #2: Hey, news peoples!! *walks over to the camera man* I saw the whole thing and my grandbaby got it all on camera too.

Cameraman: *Roll film* Can you tell me what happened?

    Old lady #2: I was sitting right cross there on my porch when I saw the young man come running from behind that building right there. Then immediately after I saw him, I saw the police trailing behind. The girl was sitting on her porch minding her own business. The young boy stopped running.

He screamed at the policemens. "I surrender! I can't

breathe". That's exactly when they started shooting. He tried

to run again because they started shooting at him. By this

time, he got closer to the girl and the police stop shooting.

Then that ole hot head police, Officer Paradowski, came

flying down the street like a mad man. He hopped out of the

car and just let go every bullet he owned and killed both of

em. I got the whole thing on camera too.

April 17, 2020

Mama J: Can someone please tell me they've found Keyawanna!?

Tylia: *runs into the dressing room* Mama J!!! Apparently, Larry is missing too!

Mama J: What!?

One hour before the wedding:

Larry: *pours a flute of champagne* Baby, this salad is goooood! *Buss out laughing,*

Keya: *takes the glass from Larry and takes a nice and easy sip from her glass.* Larry, can you play this song for me?

Larry: What would you like to hear, Keya?

Keya: Rufus and Chaka Khan, Sweet Thing.

Larry: Oooooh! You know I'm about to get jiggy up in here! *Speakers knocking Sweet Thing*

The entire room was filled with a bunch of chaos. People were literally running around like maniacs trying to get ready for this wedding. Keyawanna was tired of all the drama; so she went to find Larry. They snuck out of the

279

church and made their way to the local Fuddruckers. They grabbed some cheeseburgers and champagne, and went back to the car to enjoy their meal .

Keyawanna: I'm seriously satisfied.

Larry: Me too. That burger hit the spot! I was hungry something serious!

Keyawanna: Yeah the food was good, but I'm talking about, I'm satisfied with my life. I'm marrying my best friend, my son is a successful business man, my grandson is the smartest child I know, and I'm finally financially stable. I mean, that's my definition of being successful in life. What do you think?

Larry: Keya, I think you're right. I feel like once you've found your true purpose and your true love, you're successful.

Keyawanna: I agree. Let's go back. I feel better now. Thank you, baby!

Larry: I love you!

Keyawanna: I love you more!

Keya walks in the dressing room unbothered and stress free.

Mama J: Where have you been!!?

Keyawanna: Mama J, I need you to take five deep breaths. Please? Now is a good time for you to take your seat in the sanctuary. I believe everything is under control. The wedding will begin shortly.

She walks away from her mother, and enters into her dressing room. Everyone of her bridesmaids rushed up to her, screaming to the top of their lungs!

Everybody: There you are! Where have you been? Are you okay? Keyawanna, are you crazy!? We've been looking all over for you!

Keyawanna says with a very demanding tone:

Keyawanna: Is everybody ready?

Everybody: Yes.

Keyawanna: I will be out there shortly. I'll be out shortly. Lia, please stay.

Everyone exits the dressing room, leaving Tylia and Keyawanna alone.

Keyawanna: *Putting on her gorgeous wedding dress* Girl I couldn't take all the chaos! Everybody was being all dramatic, and I just couldn't deal.

Tylia: Where did you go? *helping Keya with her dress*

Keyawanna: Me and Larry went to Dottie's , and got some salads and champagne.

Tylia: *buss out laughing* Girl!

Keyawanna: Look inside my purse. I brought you a sandwich.

Tylia: Oooo! See this is what best friends do! I'm so hungry in here!

The ceremony finally commenced We are about fifteen minutes into the ceremony .

Pastor Morris: I believe the both of you have your own personal vows. Lawrence, you may recite your love to Keyawanna.

Larry: Keyawanna Nicole, this may sound cliché, but the very moment I laid my eyes on you, I knew you were the only one for me. Being that you're a year younger than me, I truly feel like God made you out of a piece of me. Looking at you, I see a reflection of myself. Looking at you, I see my strength, my weakness, my smile, my entire heartbeat. My sweet Keyawanna, you lit a fire in my spirit that I pray is eternal. Just as The Eternal Flame represents Dr. Martin Luther King

Jr.'s idea that our love "requires a lasting personal commitment that cannot weaken when faced with obstacles." I vow to protect you the best I know how. By praying for you, rather you're up or down. I vow to honor, respect, and love you until the day God decides He's ready for me to come on home. Keyawanna Nicole, thank you! Thank you for being you! I love you, baby!

Keyawanna: *crying* I love you too, my baby.

Pastor Morris: Keyawanna, you're turn.

Keyawanna: Thank you, Pastor. Larry, you are the soul that snaps my control. You are the missing piece of the puzzle that completes my family, my happiness, and my life. God took his time to create you, with a dash of sensitivity, few cups of masculinity, and the whole bag and an half of love. I thank God for you, every time I look into your beautiful eyes and every time I'm away from you, and you cross my mind. Larry, you are my confidant. I can tell you everything and know for a fact, that it's safe with you. Larry I promise to love you and stick by your side, even through the toughest of the tough times. I'm here for you.

Pastor Morris: That was beautiful. With that being said. I now present to you Mr. Lawrence and Mrs. Keyawanna Brooks! Lawrence, you may kiss your bride.

Lawrence takes his wife in his arms and kisses her with so much passion that she gets weak in the knees. He picks her up and spins her around while still kissing her.

They make their way to the reception. Everyone is congratulating them, and they have their first dance to Avant and Keke Wyatt, My First Love.

Wait, what!?

Today's date is May 27, 2020. Lawrence and Keyawanna have enjoyed their honeymoon, in St. Lucia. Larry wants to wait for five months after the wedding to impregnate Keyawanna. He wants to enjoy every bit of his alone time with the love of his life.

Layla moved into the house in Atlanta and she's preparing to start her summer courses at SCAD. Her and G are now completely head over heels about one another. Lil G loves his "new mommy" She treats him just like Takyia treated the boys when they were younger. King Kenneth is going down the right path, so he won't give her any reason to "hate him". G's clothing line, Thoroughbred Threads, skyrocketed, and now is one of the most popular men's clothing lines all over the States. He's working on becoming global.

Darius has won award after award for his music. He is recognized as being the most "woke" rapper in the game. He's a role model for the rappers already in the game, and now he's starting his own program. His goal is to encourage people to stop abusing drugs, focus on becoming the person that God intended them to be, and manage their money more intelligently. Darius says his goal is to make the statement "never broke again" an understatement. He's working on having legacy money. He wants to set his great grandchildren's grandchildren up for life.

Darnell Jr. still hasn't found a wife, but he's okay with that, because he knows God is going to send the woman He created specifically for him, in due time. In the meantime, he's focused on family and business.

Darriah is working to set up a meeting with Plantonic, a plane manufacturer to create the Mallane! Oh, and one last thing, Darnell and Brenda are expecting a baby!

To be continued...

Made in the USA
Columbia, SC
07 August 2024

39669458R10159